Ondřej Kundra

Vendulka
Flight
to Freedom

Translated from the Czech
by Gerald Turner

Karolinum Press

KAROLINUM PRESS is a publishing department of Charles University
Ovocný trh 560/5, 116 36 Prague 1, Czech Republic
www.karolinum.cz

Originally published in Czech as *Vendulka. Útěk za svobodou,*
Prague: Paseka, 2019

Text © Ondřej Kundra, 2021
Translation © Gerald Turner, 2021
Photography © author's archive and Jan Lukas – heirs, 2021

Cover and Design by Zdeněk Ziegler
Set and printed in the Czech Republic by Karolinum Press
First English edition

Cataloging-in-Publication Data is available from the National
Library of the Czech Republic

ISBN 978-80-246-4653-4
ISBN 978-80-246-4654-1(pdf)
ISBN 978-80-246-4656-5 (epub)
ISBN 978-80-246-4655-8 (mobi)

Contents

Together for the Last Time

Jan Lukas hung around at the Vogls' until late into the night. Dinner was mostly a silent affair, with almost no one saying a word. Then Karla started to pack their things – a maximum of 50 kilos and two pieces of luggage per person, as stated in the official instructions – and Jan took out his camera. Usually he tried to compose his shots in daylight, but it was already dark; it was still only March and sunset came early. He therefore reluctantly unpacked his flashgun and attached it to his camera. He then focused his lens and pressed the shutter release.

In the first photo, Vendulka is sitting with her mother at the dining table, which is covered in what looks like the contents of a chest of long-concealed treasures. There are soaps, medicines manufactured by the Rico company, sugar lumps, and family valuables. Karla is putting something into a paper bag, while her husband Šimon is leaning over, reading the label on a bottle. Maybe he is checking the "use by" date. They are all deeply engrossed in this odd activity. It resembles a family workshop or a stocktake in a general store.

The following shot is one that Jan Lukas decided to compose. He took a long time trying to find the right angle, until he eventually asked for a step ladder and stood on the bottom rung. Here Karla, Šimon and their daughter are already wearing their overcoats, and their belongings are packed into suitcases. Šimon has a scarf round his neck and is wearing a modern cap reminiscent of the kind favoured by his working-class neighbours in Žižkov. Vendulka is wearing knitted gloves, a three-quarter length coat, and a dress with a small check. At first glance they are an educated middle-class family. But there are disturbing details and so much tension. Šimon's hands are clenched. His wife and daughter have downcast eyes, gazing somewhere into emptiness in the corner of the room. And of course there are the white labels with numbers and the Stars of David sewn onto their coats.

Shortly afterwards Jan Lukas pressed his shutter release a third time. This time his photo captured Vendulka on her own. A moment before he had rounded on her for running around the apartment and constantly laughing at something. There was such a hustle and bustle that she had the feeling there was some adventure in store for her. "Don't you realise how serious this is?" Vendulka was taken aback by Jan's words, and froze. Nobody had ever raised their voice to her before. A moment later the camera shutter clicked. It was the last ever photograph of Vendulka together with her parents.

Meeting in Columbus

The flight from Washington to here takes two and a quarter hours. The road from the airport is lined with tall concrete buildings and warehouses. These eventually disappear and there is more greenery, but the flat Ohio landscape looks bleak and featureless nonetheless. The dark band of asphalt stretches endlessly to the horizon, and it feels as if we are pushing it away from us all the time. When we eventually drive into a residential area of the city of Columbus I am surprised to find we have suddenly arrived. We stand in front of a spacious house clad in light-coloured stones and with a massive chimney. It is surrounded by mature maple trees and shrubs. As it is winter they are now bare, but I can imagine how pleasant it must be to enjoy their shade in the summer when everything is in bloom. So this is the residence of the woman I had been seeking for several years. And even when I finally found her, it took me several more years to convince her to give me an interview. Each time she refused. Now I am turning up unannounced. Maybe it's impertinent, but I want to give it a try. For the last time.

For me this story began six years ago, when I reached on the family bookshelves for a slim volume of photographs by the Czechoslovak photographer Jan Lukas. I looked at the photos one by one until I came upon a portrait of a girl in a three-quarter-length coat. A white label with the identification number 671 hung from a string around her neck and her coat bore a star of David. I was fascinated by that strangely distant, withdrawn expression: her face intimately lit and turned to the side. As if she was turning away from something. As I later discovered, her name was Hana Vendula Voglová. She was twelve years old when the photo was taken. Jan Lukas photographed her just before she left for concentration camp. He entitled the photo simply: "Before the transport". She would subsequently become an iconic symbol of the Holocaust, which journeyed to every corner of the globe, being featured on the front pages of newspapers in various countries, and is now exhibited at the Yad Vashem Holocaust Remembrance Centre in Israel. It always interested me to know why this photo in particular. Because of the striking look of apprehension in her eyes? Or maybe because her pretty face, elegant clothes, and neatly brushed hair with that intimate lighting were in stark contrast with the horror and madness that she and her parents would undergo, along with millions of other Jews?

I couldn't tear myself away from that photograph. I wondered what happened after the shot was taken. Was the girl still alive? And if she was, how had she managed to survive? What might she look like today? She would be over seventy – how would her face have changed?

First I managed to find Jan Lukas's younger daughter Helena. She revealed to me the name of the girl in the photograph, and told me she lived in the USA. Their families had been friends after the war and she was well acquainted with her. At the same time she warned me that Vendulka never talked about what happened to her, neither to her, nor to her children. "My father always took great care that her name should never be mentioned in connection with his photograph," she told me. "It was something she didn't want." For the same reason, she refused to give me Vendulka's phone number, and only revealed her email address. And so I wrote to her for the first time in February 2014.

Dear Mrs Voglová,
You don't know me, but I take the liberty of invading your privacy and contacting you. My name is Ondřej Kundra and I have worked for the past twelve years for the weekly magazine Respekt, which was founded after the revolution by a group of dissidents associated with President Václav Havel. I am the political editor and chiefly write about Czech politics and corruption, focusing on investigative articles. I recently came across a book at home with photographs by Jan Lukas, whose work I admire. The photo that particularly stood out from all the others was the one depicting you. I keep on coming back to it and wondering what you must have gone through after it was taken, and what you must

have had to overcome. Some of my relatives were in concentration camp and my wife comes from a Jewish family, which is another reason why your portrait by Jan Lukas is of particular interest to me. Quite recently I discovered that you are living in the USA, so I decided to contact you and ask whether you might be willing to tell your story.

You could, of course, argue that the photograph speaks for itself. However, I fear that for the younger generation the Holocaust is simply past history already. They just register it as awful pictures from somewhere in the distant past. Maybe that is why anti-Semitic or generally xenophobic attitudes persist or are even being revived among some of them. For that reason I am convinced of the need to go on telling stories that recall that insane period when things were out of control, so that it should never be repeated.

With deep respect,
Yours,

Ondřej Kundra
February 2014

An answer arrived a few days later.

Dear Mr Kundra,
It is complicated, and I won't bother you with explanations. It is just that those unimaginable horrors that we lived through, and above all survived, left scars on us all that will never be healed. Some are able to speak or write about it, which is right, so that it is not forgotten. Others aren't capable – and I am one of them. As far as my photo is concerned, I always thought that it didn't have much to do with me, but chiefly with Jan Lukas, who risked his life to document some of the savagery of war.

I was twelve at the time, so I saw everything through the eyes of a child, which was maybe just as well. It was a long while before I discovered from a TV program here that only a few of the many thousands of children that passed through Terezín and went from there like me to other concentration camps, survived. I could only talk about the others with my mother or with those who had suffered a similar fate. I have read lots of excellent books written by people who were able to write.

(11)

Whatever I could tell with the best of intentions will not change the views of those who say that the Holocaust didn't exist. Please don't take offence. I know you mean well, but it simply left open wounds in those of us who were lucky enough to survive. Normal life is only possible for me if I avoid thinking about what happened. It's not possible to forget, but thinking about it as little as possible is something I can do.

Yours, Vendula Old

Every time I travelled to the USA in subsequent years, I would contact Vendulka Voglová but each time I received a warm but negative response. So I cheekily decided to simply turn up on her doorstep.

It is February 2017. A week ago I left for the USA to as part of a scholarship programme that happened to take me here to the capital of Ohio State. I would have regretted not attempting to contact her directly. I set off up the front path, imagining how she would probably react to finding me outside her door, and I prepared an apology in my mind. Will she be cross? Or will she receive me with indulgence? I pressed the copper button of the doorbell. Silence. No sound of footsteps, nor a call for me to wait a moment. Even when I pressed the bell a second time, no one came to the door. I spent a moment or two glancing around me and walking round the outside of the house, until I finally returned to the hotel disappointed.

I spent a few hours pacing up and down my hotel room. In a couple of days I was supposed to fly to California and I didn't know what to do. Several times I keyed Vendulka's phone number into my mobile (she had revealed it to me in one of her emails) and then erased it. Finally I called her number. After all, what is more impertinent – ringing her doorbell, or phoning her? After a while, a pleasant, deep voice was heard at the other end:

"Wendy Old, how can I help you?"

She once wrote to me that if I wanted to write about Jan Lukas and not about her, she might be willing to share her recollections of him. After she introduced herself on the phone, I reminded her of what she had said, and asked her to let me visit her. The other end of the phone fell silent, a silence that seemed to me endless. "OK, seeing that you've considered coming this far...," Vendulka conceded and fell silent against. "Come here tomorrow at four in the afternoon. I'll be expecting you."

I feared she would be severe and apprehensive, and keep her distance. But her reception was friendly. She was amiable, and she resonated calm, and even a kind of acceptance. She kept on apologising for her Czech, although there was no need. Lines had already transformed her face, but she looked young and elegant for her age. Her hair was tinted and carefully groomed. She invited me into the living room. Classical music was playing softly. There was a baby grand piano, and the walls were decorated with Impressionist paintings of Paris.

"It's divinely peaceful here," she said when we sat down at table. "I like it when it's warm. I sit outside under the trees and read books or draw in my studio. I've also got a large library, quite a few of the books are Czech. I try to keep up that beautiful language. "You know," she said, leaning back in her armchair, "in spite of everything I went through, I've had a beautiful life. That's in fact why I finally decided to talk to you about it. In spite of the fact that I have so far kept a lot of things from my own children."

A Prayed-for Baby

In the ideal world that we can all imagine but never build, Czechoslovakia in those days was not the best solution for the nations living on its territory during the years 1918–1938. They demanded far more than the republic gave them, and they also demanded what the republic could not give them without jeopardising its existence. Masaryk didn't rule "with a rose as a sceptre" as the poet wrote, but after him a much harder sceptre was being prepared for Europe. In the light of what we now know about what happened next, we must conclude that it would have been advantageous if Masaryk's republic had had the opportunity to continue a while longer and develop in peace.

History denied it that opportunity. It was in a dangerous location and it came to an end in an eruption a year after Masaryk's death. At the foot of the volcano it ensured its citizens a fairly protected and calm existence, at least until the lava started to flow. At a time before the advent of industrially organized murder, Masaryk failed to foresee the worst possible outcome. It was still not foolish to believe, as he did, that one nation cannot club another nation to death with hammers. When one nation really did attempt this, but with guns and Zyklon B gas instead of hammers, Masaryk was no longer alive.

Jiří Kovtun, *Republika v nebezpečném světě*
(The Republic in a Dangerous World)

Vendulka's birth on 27 December 1930 filled her parents with a sense of enormous gratification, as they had had been trying for a child for many years. Šimon was forty and Karla twenty-seven. They gave their only child the names Hana Vendula. Up to the end of the war she herself only used her first name; she became

Vendulka after the war when she wanted to start a new life and forget about the bad things in her past.

Both parents were from Jewish families, but tended to live their faith informally. They attended the synagogue irregularly but kept up Jewish traditions and culture. When Vendulka was born they were living in Karlovy Vary. Šimon had moved there on account of his work – he held a high post in the civil service as post office commissioner. The family could therefore afford to rent an apartment in a large house in the town centre, which was shared with their maid and nurse Emílie, and to own a motor car, which was still something enjoyed only by wealthier sections of the population.

Vendulka thus grew up in fairly luxury surroundings and a loving atmosphere that was almost over-indulgent. During her early years, her father taught her at home because he wanted her to get the best education. And when she later started to attend the local school, he arranged for a phone booth to be erected half-way to the school, from which she had to call home regularly to let them know she was alright. Her father's excessive attention was no doubt due to the fact that she was an only child, but his stubbornness also played a role. When he set his mind on something, there was no way of talking him out of it.

At the time the Vogls moved to Karlovy Vary (Karlsbad, in German) it was a favourite destination for enterprising and well-to-do Jewish families. The local Jewish community expanded quickly from the mid-19th century and in time constituted almost one tenth of the town's population. They contributed to the development of the spa and its amenities. Ludwig Moser's firm brought international fame to local glassmaking, and the Maier company did the same for Karlovy Vary porcelain, while the banker Alfred Schwalb helped found the luxury Hotel Imperial. As an international destination renowned for its tolerance, Karlovy Vary actually hosted two international congresses of the Zionist movement in the 1920s. Delegates from Jewish communities all over the world debated there the shape of their future state, and one of the congresses was chaired by Chaim Weizmann, who would become the first President of the State of Israel.

In spite of the Great Depression, economic development was maintained in the 1930s, and a number of costly projects were successfully completed. The most extensive of them was the dam on the river Teplá at Březová, which removed the threat of flooding from the spa. The spa's capacity was increased by a number of modern buildings; the health insurance building was built, and a technically advanced reinforced concrete bridge was erected spanning the river Ohře in the direction of the Upper Rail Station. Vendulka's father was indirectly involved in all those projects as the supplier of telephone communications.

Šimon Vogl's job with the post office gave him a comforting sense of security for life. Whereas many people lost their jobs during the Depression, he had no need to worry. On weekends he and Karla would take Vendulka on trips to the nearby Ore Mountains, where in the summer he would enjoy his hobby of photographing nature, and in the winter the family would go skiing. If they stayed in town they would take a Sunday walk in the colonnade and listen to the colonnade orchestra.

Šimon and Karla Vogl were known as a fun-loving couple and had quite a number of friends in the town. They had regular visitors at home and over afternoon coffee or tea they would discuss politics, the arts, and the latest world news. A regular guest was the successful young photographer Jan Lukas. He made the Vogls' acquaintance through his family's cook, who knew Karla Voglová. From her early childhood Vendulka regarded Lukas as part of the household. She could not even remember when he first appeared. He had simply always been there.

She always called him familiarly "Honza", but used the formal mode of address when talking to him. He was fifteen years her senior, but the age gap never constituted a barrier between them. When he didn't happen to be in conversation with her parents, he would play with her and explain to her how to use a camera, and in return she would show him her drawings. The day would come – after they had been separated by World War II, the Communist dictatorship and the Soviet occupation – when they would meet again on the other side of the world and remember with laughter those afternoons spent together.

Vendulka's birth filled her parents with a great sense of satisfaction. (Hana Vendulka Voglová, no date, archive of the Hořava and Old families)

A happy life… (with her parents in Karlovy Vary, no date, archive of the Hořava and Old families)

...with a friend and her dog Belinka. (no date, archive of the Hořava and Old families)

Budding Reporter

Jan Lukas was naturally familiar with František Drtikol's experiments with light, and also with his nude photographs, in which the curved shapes of the female body were transformed into sea waves. He also knew of Josef Sudek's poetical photographic studies and the avantgarde photographic works of Jaromír Funke. But their photographs did not really reflect real life and the real world that was changing so fast and radically at the beginning of the 20th century. Jan Lukas was attracted by something else: the present, people in the natural surroundings of their everyday lives.

In a rare interview in 1988 that he gave in New York to the writer Iva Pekárková for *Západ* magazine, a publication for Czech and Slovak emigrants, he described his approach in the following way:

"I deny that photography has anything in common with visual art. It has more in common with literature, with epics... They are something like individual anecdotes... A good photograph is one that you remember.... For that reason you don't have to print it over and over again, because once you've heard an anecdote, you don't need to hear it again. I mean to say that it is not something eternal like a painting, but more like a newspaper article."

The most precise description of Lukas is by one of his friends, the poet and translator Emanuel Frynta. (Lukas took a witty portrait of him in 1962: Frynta is standing inside a hollowed-out lime tree; only the top half of his body is visible through a hole in the trunk and he gazes straight into the camera through round-framed spectacles. It is reminiscent of devotional paintings fixed to trees at crossroads.) Frynta wrote:

"Lukas is a photographer with a keen eye. His strength is definitely not in preparation and contemplation. He understands the dynamic and flow of reality and captures the essence in an instant. The first moment is the right one for him. That's why he says reportage is the pinnacle of photographic art, by which he means quickly grasping the meaning in an unpredictable state of captivation and amazement. He thinks in thousandths of a second to understand history."

He received his first camera from an uncle at the age of twelve: a twin-lens reflex made by the German firm Rolleiflex. It was a massive angular instrument, whose viewfinder was opened by raising a hinged lid on the top, revealing an image on a ground-glass screen that is laterally inverted (i.e. left-right). It took a little while for one to get used to this looking-glass world. From then on Jan Lukas documented everything he saw around him: his friends, women stopping to chat on the street, villagers carrying bundles of sticks on their backs...

He would use his pocket money to buy magazines, which increasingly featured photos in the early twenties. He first came across them in the doctor's waiting room when going for medical checks. He was taken most by the work of André Kertész and Brassaï, avantgarde photographers of Hungarian origin. He was probably particularly impressed by their empathy and attention to chance moments in human life, when they would reveal its fragility, poetry, ludicrousness, or vulnerability, that thousandth of a second of eternity that Emanuel Frynta wrote about.

It was a splendid time for photography. Technology was improving and becoming increasingly accessible all the time. The huge large-format cameras were giving way to small portable cameras such as the German Rolleiflex, and with the invention of the 135 film cassette, photography finally wrenched itself out of the jealous hands of professionals and countless amateurs.

Avantgarde artists continued to champion it as an art medium, but Jan's generation, which was coming of age in the 1930s, no longer wanted to consider photography as a special kind of painting. What they looked for in it was poetry, a footnote, a story. Hence it was increasingly used by journalism. In the 1930s, Czechoslovakia was literally inundated with new lifestyle magazines with large photographs. With increased wealth, the middle class wanted to read about life's pleasures, look at beautiful young women, sportsmen, and people holidaying on the beach. Among young people photography was a trendy activity, and Jan Lukas was successful at it even before he reached adulthood.

In 1930, at the age of fifteen, Jan sent a few of his photos from a holiday in Italy to a photo competition organised by the Kodak company, and he came sixth. This spurred him to go on creating, and two years later he became the youngest member of the prestigious Czech Amateur Photographers' Club that operated from Nekázanka Street in Prague. They had to make an exception on Jan's account as he was not yet of age, and his parents even had to sign a statement confirming that they would "pay for any damage caused by their son". He was the baby among the forty-year-old photographers, who included, for instance, Karel Hájek, a bon vivant, who seldom missed a social or political event, the unsentimental realist Václav Jírů, who couldn't stand photography being portrayed as art, and the inveterate experimenter Jiří Jeníček. But it was Karel Hájek, above all, that the young photographer would remember. A tall, hefty man (Jan would refer to him in the above-mentioned conversation as that "enormous guy") who earned his living as a tram driver. In his free time he would photograph his friends' weddings, and they would work his shifts in return. He would regularly have his large-format Mentor camera with him when driving his tram. The moment he saw an interesting scene or moment, he would stop and leave the tram in the middle of street while he took some photos.

In short, the club in Nekázanka Street spawned cheerful young men who passionately debated their achievements, lapped up French photography, and saw photography as the medium of the future. Jan Lukas couldn't get enough of their perceptions and he started to feel the world was their oyster. He was still at school, and he enrolled in a commercial academy at his father's request. But on his way to school he would pass shop windows with magazines that featured his photos on their covers. If he had restricted himself to what his parent's wished, he would never have become a photographer.

He came from a middle-class family. His father was a chicory salesman and later worked for the private firm of Franck selling coffee. Like Vendulka's family, the Lukases owned a car, rented an apartment, and could afford a domestic help. No wonder

Jan's father wanted a similar career for his son, and at first he was not particular taken by his son's hobby. At a time when a job was for life, photography seemed to him to offer an uncertain career with an irregular income, apart from its suspect avantgarde connotations. So it took Jan's first successes, when his work was accepted by the editors of Prague magazines and newspapers, to make his parents gradually change their minds. But the journalists were convinced that the young photographer was simply a messenger boy, and kept on asking when they would finally get to see the real author of the photos he brought. They thought they were the work of Jan's father.

The Nekázanka club had all the latest technology. Jan had access to a studio with a large camera, six darkrooms for developing films, and six with photographic enlargers. The premises were always packed, and the photographers went in one after another. He would therefore always creep into the darkrooms on a Friday before the cleaner arrived. This meant he secretly had to cut classes at school. But the hours he spent incognito in the darkroom paid off. He was perfecting his skills, and with the help of recommendations from more experienced colleagues, his photos were finding their way into popular magazines such as *Eva* or the Sunday *Ahoj*.

When he wasn't taking photos, he would spend his free time at Voskovec and Werich's "Liberated Theatre". He got to like swing, with its scintillating dynamics, drive and rhythm. He enjoyed to the full the freedom he could afford thanks to his photographic fees. He documented the life of people in southern Bohemia, where he was born, and he made trips to Moravia and Slovakia. In 1935 he even travelled to Estonia and Norway, and spent the following years in Vienna, where he studied graphic design. His career seemed to be full of all the optimism and hopes of the new republic.

He had his first successful exhibition in the spring of 1936. It was held at Prague's Mánes Gallery where he featured alongside top photographers from home and abroad, including Man Ray, Lászlo Moholy-Nagy, Alexander Rodchenko, Josef Sudek, Jaromír Funke, and Jindřich Štyrský. Entitled prosaically *The International Exhibition of Photography*, the show nonetheless attracted almost ten thousand visitors in under a month. As a result, Jan

Lukas was finally able to convince his parents that the profession he dreamed of had real prospects.

Following his studies in Vienna, Jan was selected by visionary businessman Jan Antonín Baťa for a film crew making commercials for the Baťa footwear company in Zlín. Baťa had set up a film studio and sent his people to the USA on fact-finding tours to draw inspiration and learn the latest advertising techniques. Jan Lukas was new to cinematography and had to hit the ground running. And once more he proved himself. Together with the director and future lifelong friend Alexander Hackenschmied he helped produce their breakthrough advertisement for motor car tyres *The Road Sings*, which was awarded a Gold Medal at the Paris World Fair in 1937.

However, composing scenes and having to keep a constant eye on the actors' performances and the lighting were not really his thing. Photography fascinated him for totally different reasons. He was interested in the unrepeatable instant, the miraculous spark to be glimpsed in the commonplace, the game of chance which was just as important for him in his reporting as the art of looking. And so in his free time he would dash around Zlín photographing everything he found: May Day celebrations, swimming and sporting events, workers, Antonín Baťa boarding a plane to fly round the world...

During the thirties other themes started to appear among his photographs: men in lederhosen and long white socks, swastikas daubed on walls, broken Jewish gravestones...

Understanding the dynamic of reality. (Young people's summer frolics, Norway, 1935, photo Jan Lukas)

Capturing everyday life... (Václav Luzůn's family, Moravia, 1936, photo Jan Lukas)

...and key moments of Czech history. (Jan Lukas with Alexandr Hackenschmied, 1935, Zlín, archive of Helena Lukas)

And Then the War Began

In those days it was as if everyone had come down with a fever. World War I had left behind ten million dead and 20 million wounded, and until recently it seemed unthinkable that the Germans would want to provoke a conflict of such proportions again. Mud, typhus and rats in the trenches at Ypres, mustard gas penetrating uniforms and slowly corroding lungs, the blood-soaked fields of Flanders, the heroic but desperate battle of Czechoslovak units at Sochi and Piava... these were all still fresh in the collective memory. But humiliation, the sense of superiority, and anger would once more set the wheels of history in motion.

The economic and political crisis in Europe after 1929 undermined confidence in liberal democracy, and a yearning for a new order grew in strength. The parties of extreme right and left rejected democracy and gained support through populist promises to bring a radical solution to the crisis. Whereas Hitler only obtained 2.8% of the votes in the 1928 general election, his score had risen to 37% by the federal elections of July 1932. Woodrow Wilson's optimistic forecast that the post-war world would be safe for democracy turned out to be a naïve wish. Most of the democracies established in Europe after 1918 gave way to authoritarian regimes, and even in Czechoslovakia, the most liberal state of central Europe, the situation was far from ideal.

For instance, the Constitution had been adopted without representation of the Sudeten Germans, and opened with the words: "We, the Czechoslovak nation". Czech and Slovak became the official languages of the state, and the ethnic Germans could only use German in official communications in regions where they constituted over 20% of the population. Most of them were never reconciled with the creation of Czechoslovakia, particularly after the land reform, which deprived the richest German farmers of much of their land. The Germans' feeling of playing second fiddle in the new republic was exacerbated by the Great Depression, which became fertile soil for extremism. The National Socialists, who usually won over ten percent of the votes of the ethnic Germans, grew stronger. They organised self-confident rallies, and provoked strikes and skirmishes.

Although the Czechoslovak government banned the DNSAP – the German National Socialist Workers Party – after the Nazis came to power in Germany in 1933, there arrived on the scene Konrad Henlein, the 35-year-old son of a Czech mother, who founded the Sudeten German Patriot Front (subsequently renamed the Sudeten German Party – SdP), in which he managed to unite both moderate and extreme wings of German nationalism. In 1935, his party received the highest number of votes, and the SdP became the strongest party in Czechoslovakia. Henlein's militia later started to harass and attack their opponents in the border areas – Czechs, Jews and German social democrats.

Hence some historians would later maintain that there were not two world wars but rather one unending conflict with temporary pauses, which enabled some breathing space.

Vendulka was unaware of any of this. She was still a little girl and, moreover, a single child of a wealthy family. Her parents protected her from the growing animosity of their German neighbours or classmates. One event did imprint itself on her memory, however. On 14 September 1937, Tomáš Garrigue Masaryk died. His funeral took place seven days later. The coffin with the remains of the first president of Czechoslovakia, covered with the national flag, was loaded onto a gun-carriage drawn by six horses and slowly passed through the streets of the capital. The funeral procession was headed on horseback by General Jan Syrový, followed by soldiers marching with their banners, a contingent of legionaries, and members of the Sokol gymnastics association. Walking behind the coffin were the president's son Jan, and his grandchildren, together with Masaryk's successor Edvard Beneš, members of the government, and representatives of European countries.

Respectful silence reigned in the Vogl home. The entire family sat together by the radio and listened to the broadcast. At that moment the funeral procession had reached the Wilson Station where a special funeral train was standing. The coffin was placed on a catafalque in the middle coach of the train. The presidential coach was attached to the end of the train. In it sat Jan Masaryk with the late president's grandchildren, and President Beneš with his entourage. The funeral train then set off for the presidential country retreat at Lány, where the first president was buried to the strains of his favourite folk song *Ach synku, synku.* As a democrat and patriot, Vendulka's father was an admirer of Masaryk. During the radio broadcast he sighed several times, saying: "Masaryk's death means the end of the First Republic."

What Vendulka observed as a small child and now recalled only vaguely, Jan Lukas documented at close range. Two years before the death of Masaryk, he had taken a portrait of the first Czechoslovak president at Lány, and now he was photographing the procession that accompanied his coffin on his last journey through Prague. On one of his photos he symbolically prefigured the transmutation of the First Republic into the Second Republic. It is a gloomy image taken in early morning: a gun-carriage with Masaryk's coffin stands in a paved courtyard. Day is breaking and the street lamps are still alight. In the foreground Edvard Beneš, the new president of Czechoslovakia, stands with his hands clasped, like a sentinel. It is clear from Lukas's photos of the period that he was aware of the growing anger and anxiety among people. He was a photo-reporter, after all, and it was he who helped establish photo journalism as a genre in the Czech lands. He sensed the growing danger in Europe and was very close to it on several occasions.

On 25 July 1934, just a year before he left for graphic design school in Vienna, members of the SS-Standarte 89 unit murdered the Austrian chancellor, Engelbert Dollfuss. It was a revenge assassination for his outright rejection of the merger of Austria and Germany, and for his outspoken criticism of the Nazi movement. On that fateful morning, 143 men, headed by the commander of the Nazi putschists, Otto Planetta, burst into the Chancellery and shot the Austrian leader twice in the neck. Engelbert Dollfuss bled to death. The putschists refused the dying Chancellor medical assistance or a priest.

After the chancellor's death, Austria managed to resist the growing might of Nazism, but four years later it submitted voluntarily to Hitler's Germany. The events of the so-called Anschluss are documented, for instance by the American historian Timothy Snyder in his book *Black Earth*, which records the experience of a Jew, Erika M.

It happened on Saturday, 11 March 1938. Orthodox Jews interrupted their Sabbath that day to listen to the speech in which the new Chancellor Schuschnigg announced his decision not to defend Austria from Hitler. The next morning "scrub groups" (Reibpartien) appeared on the streets of Vienna. Members of the Austrian Nazi paramilitary SA had rounded up Jews on the basis of lists and forced them kneel on the pavement and scrub the paving stones. In his book Snyder quotes a journalist who described the deranged atmosphere of those days:

"...the fluffy Viennese blondes, fighting one another to get closer to the elevating spectacle of the ashen-faced Jewish surgeon on hands and knees before a half-dozen young hooligans with Swastika armlets and dog-whips."

Jan Lukas arrived in Vienna a few weeks later. By then Austria had been occupied by units of the German Wehrmacht. His photo reportage includes two particularly eloquent photos. One of them shows an advertising column with a poster of Hitler's portrait and the slogan *Ein Volk – Ein Reich – Ein Führer*, and beneath it a poster announcing the performance of a play entitled *The Good Old Times*. On another of his photos Jan Lukas managed to take a shot of German officers with a swastika flag hanging behind them.

"We'll be in Prague this time next year," one of them told him. He had noticed he was being photographed and asked where the young photographer was from. "What are you going to do about it?" the officer added arrogantly.

"We'll fight," Lukas replied, at which the Nazi officer burst out laughing. Czechs were not the first to flee the Sudetenland, but rather German anti-fascists and social democrats who risked injury or even death at the hands of the extremist members of the SdP and its paramilitary Freikorps. After 23 September 1938, when SdP violence had escalated into an attempted putsch, the Czechoslovak government declared a state of emergency, and twenty thousand of them fled inland.

"These are all people of German nationality, who have demonstrated in a drastic – and for them grievous – fashion what they think of the swastika-mongers," wrote the daily *České slovo*. By then Vendulka and her parents were living in Prague, having left Karlovy Vary in mid-September. It was no longer safe for Jews to go out after dark, as units of the Freikorps were even starting to attack police stations. The Vogls were fortunate in being one of the wealthier Jewish families, so they could afford to leave. They had somewhere to go to and were able to provide for themselves in internal exile.

Šimon Vogl sent Vendulka ahead with her nursemaid Emilka to stay with his wife's parents, who owned a house at 173 Milíčova Street in Prague's Žižkov district. They had bought it in 1917 with money they had saved from trading in eiderdown fillings.

As state employees, Šimon and his wife were evacuated several days later. They took with them just family valuables and their dog Belinka; everything else they left in the Karlovy Vary apartment. They were reluctant to leave, but the spa town had long ceased to be the pleasant, cosmopolitan resort beneath the slopes of the Ore Mountains, whose Czech, German and Jewish inhabitants had lived in relative calm, and which was a favoured destination for tourists from half of the globe for its peaceful atmosphere.

Vendulka was not initially taken with the Žižkov district. She had no friends there, and did not know her way around the streets, which were almost unpleasantly busy and overcrowded. It was as if there was no indication that a war would break out in a few weeks. Žižkov's main thoroughfares – Karlova and Husova streets – were crammed with shops. It was a place where prams, musical instruments, paper hats, clothing, gloves, toys, chocolate and other foods were manufactured and sold. Shop windows lured passers-by with brightly coloured advertisements, and neon signs shone above the wealthier stores. Built on a hill, Žižkov housed a number of essential oil factories or electrical goods works, and Prokop Square was a well-known market place. Vendulka would go shopping there with her mother, and on weekends they would sometimes go to the cinema together to lift their spirits in their new surroundings, and, for a short while, to forget what was going on in the Czech border country.

Jan Lukas spent that period mostly in the streets. In his photographs, scenes of carefree everyday life gave way to shots documenting the fast-moving events of those days...

23 September 1938
A portrait of President Edvard Beneš at his desk, surrounded by heaps of official files. Maybe he has just finished signing the order for mobilisation.

24 September 1938
Helmeted Czechoslovak soldiers marching determinedly in ranks with rifles over their shoulders. A bristling forest of bayonets. Jan Lukas took the shot from a very low angle, which lends a sense of menace to the atmosphere in the photo.

1 October 1938
Three railway workers looking at a copy of the *Právo lidu* newspaper. With sombre expressions on their faces, they peruse the map of Czechoslovakia and its new frontiers dictated by the Munich Agreement. The entire border zone is ceded to Nazi Germany without a fight.

Early October 1938
Refugees from Sudetenland – two young women and a woman with little children –wait in front of a Prague shop window. The sign on the window offers an odd assortment of wares: *BUY PERSONNEL GAS MASKS WITH A FILTER AND BOX.*

The first place Adolf Hitler headed for to celebrate his success was Karlovy Vary, where Vendulka was born. His arrival was recorded by the American journalist Vincent Sheean, who spent the 1930s in Europe and collaborated with the Czech cameraman Alexander Hackenschmied and with Jan Lukas on the documentary film Crisis, describing the upheavals of those days. He stayed in a hotel by the municipal gardens. The day before the arrival of the Nazi leader, a strange scene played itself out in front of his window. A team of men, women and children suddenly appeared from nowhere and started tearing out of the ground all the flowers, rose bushes, and saplings. Initially he thought it was the first sign of looting following the departure of Czechoslovak troops from the town, but then he realised that the local Germans were simply clearing the space for the crowd that Hitler would address. Sheean's account of the subsequent events is unique and so compelling that it is worth quoting at length:

> The army began to enter in force before ten o'clock, big lorries filled with infantrymen and machine gunners. The bonnets of their cars were festooned with flowers; they had flowers on their rifles and helmets; all the girls in the streets reached out eagerly to touch their hands as the trucks passed. (...) By now the loudspeakers were announcing Hitler's progress from Eger, point by point, interspersing these bits of interesting information with advice and orders to the crowd. It rained intermittently during the morning, and the first crowds in the Schmuckplatz put up their umbrellas. The loudspeaker admonished them about this, saying that the Führer was on his way to them in an open car, unprotected against the elements, and that they should be prepared to endure a little rain while they waited for him. (...) There was a general laugh and the umbrellas went down. (...) At one-forty the loudspeakers began to fill in time by music, but ten minutes later the booming voice of the chief announcer said very solemnly: "the Führer is in Carlsbad." From then on until the great man appeared in the square, the cheering was continuous. (...) At one fifty-four exactly, preceded by a sound truck with the movie crank steadily grinding, Hitler entered the square, rigid in his long military coat and cap, his hand at the military salute. The crowds then chanted in unison (...) "Wir danken unserem Führer [We thank our Leader]." This seemed to be the principal slogan of the day, and was chanted again and again both during Hitler's speech and afterwards, alternating with the brief, savage barking noise of "Sieg Heil, Sieg Heil." (...) The Führer walked out on the balcony of the theatre, giving the Nazi salute and receiving it from the massed crowd in the square beneath. The applause – general now, not cadenced or organised, but an outburst of hysterical yells and howls – continued for exactly five minutes, after which Hitler turned it off by signaling with his hand. It's stopped as a light goes off when you turn the switch.

(...) Hitler's own speech, which followed, lasted just ten minutes. (...) The speech on the whole was calm (for Hitler) and contained only one moment of the maniacal intensity which we expected. This was when he hit the balcony rail in front of him and said: "Das ich hier ein Tag stehen würde, das hab' ich gewusst [That I would be standing here one day, that I knew]!" (...) His declaration that he had "always known it" was characteristic of the sort of lunacy which had made Hitler such an unquestionable idol to his own people. (...) There were some women in the crowd who fainted; I saw one carried out of the square and another brought into our hotel.

Hitler spent only an hour and a quarter in Karlovy Vary. He received a telegram from the foreign ministry in Berlin about complications that had arisen in the negotiations of the international commission established to decide the post-Munich frontiers of Czechoslovakia. He therefore cut short his visit. But he managed to whip up the local inhabitants to a frenzy. A month later, on 9 November 1938, "Kristallnacht" – the largest anti-Jewish pogrom since the Middle Ages – erupted in Karlovy Vary, as in other places in the Sudetenland and Germany. The pretext was the assassination of Ernst vom Rath, a secretary at the German Embassy in Paris, by a Polish Jew, Herschel Grynszpan.

The attacks on the Jewish inhabitants of Karlovy Vary was signalled by the trumpets of the Hitlerjugend. Shortly afterwards, the synagogue in Sadová Street went up in flames. It was one of the finest and largest synagogues on the territory of Czechoslovakia, where Vendulka and her parents would celebrate Hanukkah, and sometimes Pesach and Yom Kippur, as well as other Jewish festivals from time to time. Jewish hospitals and shops suffered a similar fate. Bands of four or five SA members went through the streets, which were covered in shards of glass from the broken shop windows, inciting the population to come out of their houses and join in the attacks on the Jews. They broke into the houses of 238 of the Jews who remained in the town. They literally threw them onto the backs of trucks and drove them to the police station, where they were made to stand with their faces to the wall. They were only allowed home after they had signed a paper saying they willingly surrendered their property to the Germans.

The next day, most of the Jewish families that remained in Karlovy Vary decided to flee. But now it wasn't as easy as it had been in mid-September when the Vogls left. There was only one train leaving the station, so they all tried to send their children above all to the Czech hinterland. Parents even put their children onto the train through open windows. When the train left the station it didn't stop until it reached Plzeň (Pilsen) the first main station in the truncated post-Munich Republic. Heinlein supporters with dogs were standing on the station platforms giving the Hitler salute in the villages and towns they passed through on their way.

Šimon and Karla Vogl read in the newspapers about the pogrom in Karlovy Vary. Vendulka noticed her parents grow solemn and sensed their unhappiness. Her mother cried softly, and Vendulka could also see tears in her father's eyes. She didn't realise yet how serious the situation was and she related her parents' grief to the loss of her friends and classmates and the move to Žižkov, where she did not yet feel at home, and she herself became dejected. She didn't cheer up until the Christmas tree arrived. She wanted her parents to get one, but her grandparents, who were very pious Jews, were not in favour at first. But when her grandfather saw how sad she was, he went to the market on the day before Christmas Eve and returned with an enormous tree, maybe the biggest to be had.

"It was an odd Hanukkah that time. Not only because of the Christmas tree that grandpa brought home. Everyone at our place realised that another war was coming ..."
Only when Vendulka fell silent after those words and glanced out of the window, did I realise that it was getting dark outside. It was as if we had emerged from that dark past and were suddenly once more in America at her house in Columbus.
"Would you like some tea?" she asked.
I simply nodded. The sound of her melodic voice as she told her story was still running through my head. I listened to the kettle starting to boil next door in the kitchen, and I looked around the room once more. The atmosphere was oddly old-fashioned. It felt a bit like I was sitting in the Vogls' pre-war apartment in

Žižkov. Maybe it was on account of the piano and the photos on the wall, or maybe I was just imagining it. When Vendulka came back from the kitchen, she brought with her photos of her children and grandchildren.

"That's my daughter Christina and her son Simon. He also wants to be an architect like his mother. He was named after my father. And these are my daughters Susan and Kathy and their children."

She placed a teapot in front of me, and some biscuits on a plate.

"Why did you never tell them about your life in World War II, in fact?" I asked.

"I don't know. Maybe I should have. There were several reasons, of course, but since they had grown up that time in America it seemed to me that it would sound unbelievable to them. Impossible. But you're right, I ought to talk to them about it."

It was dark outside the windows, and we once more sat down in the comfortable armchairs face to face.

"But why, Mummy? Why can't we go to the park? Why can't I take the tram to Hagibor any more?"

Karla drew Vendulka towards her and sat her on her lap. She hesitated for a moment, wondering to what extent it made sense to explain to her daughter all the events of the previous months. Why she was not allowed out after eight in the evening. Why they weren't allowed to into some streets, parks, or squares. Why they could not use public transport. Why they were enclosed in a ghetto with invisible walls.

"It was the decision of people who don't like us."

"Us. Who do you mean?"

"Us. Jews."

Masaryk's death meant the end of the First Republic. (Edvard Beneš at the funeral of T.G. Masaryk, Prague, 1937, photo Jan Lukas)

One People – One Empire – One Leader! (Advertising column
with Hitler's portrait, Vienna, 1938, photo Jan Lukas)

New times, new product range. (Displaced people from
the Sudetenland in front of a shop window advertising gas masks,
Prague, 1938, photo Jan Lukas)

(40)

Railway workers perusing a map of Czechoslovakia with its frontiers eroded by the Munich treaty. (1938, photo Jan Lukas)

A German soldier on guard in front of Prague Castle.
(1940, photo Jan Lukas)

Vendulka did come to like Žižkov in the end after all, chiefly because of the children she made friends with at her new school. But soon there were fewer and fewer places where she could meet up with them. Jewish children used to get together in the garden of the Jewish old-folks home, or at the Jewish cemeteries in Žižkov or the Old Town. But Vendulka preferred Hagibor, an area on the borders of Žižkov and Strašnice, where the Jewish community had built a sports ground. When the Protectorate was declared, it became a sort of informal centre, the last place where the Jewish inhabitants could meet freely and in safety. Apart from sport, it was a place for singing, recitation, rehearsing plays, or learning scouting skills, and every Sunday there were debates about Jewish history, Zionism, culture, and sexual issues.

The main organiser and moving spirit behind all the various activities was Fredy Hirsch, a young, athletically-built German Jew with brylcreemed hair and a strong German accent. Whereas his brother and mother had fled from the Nazis to Bolivia, he was a fervent Zionist and headed for Czechoslovakia in 1935, determined to find a new home only in Palestine. It was above all his charisma and the untiring enthusiasm and warmheartedness with which he treated all children irrespective of age that allowed them to forget about the hostile world beyond the brick wall. Vendulka would often recall the favourite catch-phrases he used to raise others' spirits. "What doesn't kill me makes me stronger," he said, slapping a Jewish boy on the back when he arrived in tears because his former German classmates had beaten him up. "Do you know what Hagibor means? It's Hebrew for hero." – "Where there's a will there's a way," he would say cheerfully when one of his charges succeeded in something.

Volleyball was Vendulka's favourite activity. She would spend almost every afternoon at Hagibor with friends. Once she interrupted her everyday routine in order to escape with her friend Dita Krausová to a photographic studio on the street Na Příkopě, where they had twenty-four portraits taken of themselves from various angles and printed on one large sheet. It was all the rage at the time, like autograph books would be later. They then cut out the separate photos and shared them with their friends. Just a few months later it was forbidden to serve Jews in shops.

The first anti-Jewish measures were introduced by the Czech government soon after the signing of the Munich Agreement in September 1938. They were not legal norms like the Nuremberg Laws – being framed in national, not racial terms – but the effect was almost the same. The Czechoslovak Medical Association, the Chamber of Civil Engineers, and the Czech Lawyers Association demanded that members of Jewish nationality be banned from their professions in order to eliminate competition. The following quotation is eloquent testimony to it:

"To the highly esteemed government of the Czecho-Slovak government," a Dr Bohumil Šedivý a from Plzeň addressed a letter in which he "respectfully" requested "a resolution of the Jewish question". The thirty-one-year-old lawyer would seem to have intended it quite innocently. He wanted to open his own practice, but the number of lawyers in his town had increased to such an extent that they couldn't all make a living, according to him. Over half of them were "Jews", who, according to Šedivý "were not Czechs", who "never felt themselves to be Czechs", and as they are "well off" he couldn't compete with them, being an "impecunious Czech probationary barrister, the son of a widow of a working man without support. If the situation doesn't change, I and my mother will have nothing to live on, let alone start a family, and I will have to look on while Jewish barristers of Jewish or German nationality make a good living in Czech Plzeň from the money of the Czech people of Plzeň."

Because of such demands, Jewish barristers, doctors and civil engineers could thenceforth only work within their own community. Even some local associations of the Czechoslovak Sokol Union called for Jews to be expelled. Jewish state employees were also given early retirement on the basis of a government decree, or they were transferred to places outside the larger towns to prevent them from influencing public opinion in any way.

The star of films in the First Republic, the actor and director Hugo Haas, was fired from the National Theatre. First he was denounced for having had the temerity to write the script for the film "Gossips" of 1938, as well as direct it and play the main role. Such creative activity should be restricted to "real Czechs and Slovaks". As an apolitical bohemian, he was stunned by such drastic treatment and he wrote a letter to the journalist Karel Horký in which he sadly gave vent to his surprise that his "self-evident Czechness" was suddenly contested and he was denied the possibility of working on the Czech cultural scene. After his dismissal he fled to Vienna and from there to America, where he continued a successful career.

When "The Bartered Bride" was performed at the National Theatre on 13 October 1938, part of the orchestra demanded that the name of the Jewish producer Hanuš Thein be removed from the posters, and they had their way. And on 28 October, an audience in Brno refused to allow the Jewish conductor Milan Sachs to conduct a performance of Smetana's opera "Libuše".

The Czech government's persecution of the Jews was even noted by the British authorities who gave financial support to Jewish families fleeing Europe to Palestine. In the end half a million pounds was given on condition that the Czech government cease discriminating against the Jews. It was only due to British pressure that 2,500 Jews were able to leave the Czech lands during the so-called Second Republic and take some of their property with them to their new home.

After the German occupation and the establishment of the Protectorate on 15 March 1939 there was no longer anywhere to escape to. The Czech lands became part of Hitler's plans for a "final solution" to the Jewish question. The Jews were outlawed and stripped of their human rights. They could not use public transport, go to the cinema, use telephone booths, shop, or leave their residence after 8 pm. In addition, as part of so-called "aryanisation", their companies were confiscated, their bank and savings books were cancelled, and fifteen thousand were evicted from their apartments, which were then taken over by German home seekers. None of the money raised from this was received by the government of the Czech protectorate government, it all went to the German Reich, which benefited to the tune of two hundred billion crowns. This was essentially money from "aryanised" Jewish firms and arms companies, which helped the Nazis unleash the World War II inferno.

The Vogls also received an eviction order in the post. They had to leave the house of Karla's parents and move into a flat in the house at 4 Lodecká Street in the Old Town. The only reason they received it was because Šimon started to work for the Prague Jewish Community, which owned the building. A corner house, it was designed by the architect and set designer František Zelenka, and it was one of only a few functionalist buildings with bands of French windows. The Vogls' flat was on the top floor.

From Vendulka's bedroom there was access to a corner balcony. She would play there with their dog Belinka, and when the weather was fine she would set up a camp-bed there and sunbathe. Almost every morning she would dash out, still in her dressing gown, and admire the view over the Vltava river.

Jan Lukas also enjoyed the panorama. He would photograph Prague from the balcony when he dropped by to see the Vogls. He lived quite nearby. After the occupation he did not return to Zlín but remained at his parents in Prague at the apartment they rented in Mělnická Street, just a few blocks away. Vendulka's mother would join him on the balcony to smoke one of her favourite slender cigarettes inserted into a metal cigarette holder. She wanted to discuss the events of recent days with him in private out of earshot of Vendulka. Unlike the Vogls, he could move around freely, so he had greater scope and was better informed. In order to be inconspicuous, he carried his camera hidden under his coat, which he would open just long enough to take a shot and then quickly hide it back in the folds of his clothes.

One can see on the photos he took at that time how the cheerful expressions of anonymous people in the street give way to glum faces and downcast eyes, hidden beneath the brims of hats. "Human hatred made itself felt. Not even the dead were spared if they were Jews," he commented about a photograph of broken Jewish gravestones.

He risked severe sanctions by visiting the Vogls. It was an offence simply to show any sympathy towards the Jews. So he was cautious, but he never stopped visiting them. On occasions he even took Vendulka to the riverside for a walk. In a small way he took her father's place after Šimon Vogl failed to return home one day.

Vendulka never did find out why the German intelligence agency, the *Sicherheitsdienst*, arrested her father. She simply knew that as a patriot he had joined the anti-Nazi resistance, most likely as a member of the *Věrni zůstaneme* (We shall remain loyal) organisation that chiefly comprised trade unionists from the post office and the railway. Following the occupation, they garnered information for the allied armies, organised clandestine border crossings, and distributed clandestine literature. That would tally with the crime with which he was charged – espionage and high treason. He was saved by his wife Karla, and by a coincidence which maybe even he did not hesitate to call divine intervention.

By various means – and thanks to bribes – Karla managed to contact the Nazi commander who had the authority to intervene in Šimon's case. When she opened the door of his office his dog rushed up to her and started to bark at her furiously. But suddenly the dog's aggressive assault changed to enraptured whining and he started to lick Karla's hands with joy. The Nazi officer could not get over his amazement. Usually the animal was aggressive towards strangers and would attack them furiously. But the dog recognised Karla Voglová as his former mistress. It was Belinka, Vendulka's dog, that she used to take with her when she went out to play in the streets of Žižkov, and onto the balcony of their apartment in Lodecká Street.

Šimon Vogl had not liked the dog because of its strident barking, so one day he drove it to some acquaintances on a farm outside the city. On that occasion Vendulka cried the whole night and refused to speak to her father for several days. How Belinka found her way to the Petschek Building, the Gestapo's headquarters, where Šimon was being held, will always remain a mystery. But now she had saved the life of her former owner. Softened by the unexpected meeting and the bribe – and no doubt aware that his Jewish opponent would not escape them in the end – the Nazi officer did as requested by Karla, and a few days later, Šimon Vogl was released.

He returned home dispirited and undernourished. He related his imprisonment in the Petschek Building with a broken voice. He said he used to work out mathematical equations in his head so as not to give in to his fear. But he didn't manage to rid himself of anxiety totally. On 1 October 1941 the first wave of Jewish residents of Prague received a white sheet of paper in their mail-boxes bearing the following official notice:

> This is to inform you that on the basis of a decree you have been assigned to a transport. Report to 3 Dlouhá Street on Friday 16.10.1941 at 12 noon with your luggage, but by 6 pm at the latest. Prepare your luggage as soon as you receive this notification. It must not exceed 50 kg in weight, i.e. a maximum of two pieces of hand luggage (NB tools, wash basins and water pails are not permitted). You must bring your luggage in person, as there will be no facilities available for them to be carried. The assembly date must be adhered to unconditionally. Participants in the transport who fail to present themselves at the appointed time will be dealt with under emergency measures.

Vendulka and her parents received their summons to join the transport the day before they were due to report: 5 March 1943. For a period they had been protected from the order to leave because Šimon was working for the Jewish community, and specifically for the checking service of the department known as *Treuhandstelle*, whose task was to liquidate the contents of sealed apartments after they were abandoned by Jews deported from Prague and the environs.

The documents in Šimon Vogl's file in the archive of the Prague Police Department reveal that as late as 1941 he applied for a clean criminal record certificate "for the purpose of an application to the American embassy". Like many other Jews who had some financial means or contacts, they were attempting to emigrate up to the last moment. The fact that they tried to emigrate to the USA in spite of the strict quotas, and in a situation that was already hopeless, is quite unusual. By that time Jews were instead "only" trying to find some way to travel to Shanghai, and most of them did not even manage to leave the country. The Vogls therefore must have had some contacts or something that gave them hope to attempt what was by then essentially impossible.

Every morning in the previous two years they had been expecting the piece of paper with the order to leave, but they were still taken by surprise when it came. At the last minute Karla gathered together confectionery, sugar lumps, honey, jam, fat, medicine and family valuables. She put everything on the kitchen table, and when there was no longer room, on the bed as well. She and Vendulka took some of the valuables out of their boxes to make them lighter, while others they put in bags to keep them dry. When they came upon a little suitcase with family photos, Šimon realised they must call Jan Lukas, so that they could say goodbye and ask him to take a photo of them all before they left. Lukas arrived a few minutes later.

"You can take the same photo in this flat when we get back," Šimon said with his arm round the photographer's shoulder. Jan Lukas took his camera out of its case and did what he had always been best at. He focussed the camera on his friends' family and in a thousandth of a second he captured them for all eternity as they were about to leave with their 50kg of possessions in suitcases.

For the last few hours remaining before their departure, Karla sent Vendulka to the neighbours on the floor below to get some sleep. She wanted her daughter to get some rest before the journey, while she herself went on packing the last few things. As Vendulka was leaving, Jan Lukas leaned down and said goodbye to her in a more intimate fashion than was their custom. To her surprise, he hugged her and kissed her on the cheek.

A short while later he was already dashing home through the darkened streets to hide the negatives. If German soldiers stopped him and found the film on him, he would have ended up in a concentration camp like the Vogls. At home he took the roll of film out of the camera, wrapped it in a rag, and placed it in a tube with a lid. He went down to the boiler room and stuck the film into a crevice in the wall behind the coal stack. Then he covered up the crevice. He knew that the coal stack would never completely disappear, as there were regular deliveries. The roll of film would remain hidden there for the rest of the war. He did not develop it until Vendulka returned from Auschwitz in 1945.

Karla woke Vendulka up a few minutes before their departure to give her time to have breakfast, and then dressed her in several layers of warm clothing. Each of them left the house with one suitcase bearing a number on a sticky label. Vendulka was assigned the number 671, her mother 670, and her father 669. Before long her shoulder was aching with the weight of the suitcase and Šimon had to help her. As they approached Bubny station, more families with suitcases like them started to appear. Most of the passers-by looked straight ahead obliviously. None of them greeted them or uttered a word of support. For Czech citizens, everyday life in the Protectorate went on as usual. In the newspaper that day there were recipes for orange desserts, and Sparta beat Slavia 4:3. In the Literary Monday section there was a review of Kamil Bednář's verse collection *Barefoot Skies*. The front page was full of Nazi propaganda about the progress of the war, but not a word about the Jewish transports, of course.

The decision that trains with Jewish prisoners would depart from Bubny station in Prague was taken shortly after Reinhard Heydrich, one of the main authors of the so-called Final Solution, was appointed Reichsprotektor. He flew into Prague at the end of September 1941 and was followed in subsequent days by eight thousand more Nazi officials and representatives of the Reich's security agencies. Heydrich needed to find accommodation for them, which the transports helped expedite. The administrative staff moved into the apartments that the Jews left behind.

As soon as he assumed office, Heydrich gave the order to find a suitable location to assemble the Jews before they were loaded onto trains. It is unclear who actually came up with the idea of Bubny, but in all events the station fulfilled all the requirements – it was not right in the centre for all to see, but nor was it very far away. Most of Prague's Jews lived in Žižkov, the Old Town, or Holešovice districts, all of which were in fairly easy walking distance. There was a vacant lot a few hundred metres from the station where they could be interned for a few days before the train departed. It was a single-storey wooden exhibition hall, known as the Radiotrh, and adjacent exhibition stands, which were originally built before the war for trade fairs to display the latest technological achievements. But Heydrich's subordinates found a completely new and unexpected use for the site. It could hold a thousand people, which was exactly the number assigned to each of the trains. Hire of the premises was paid for out of the proceeds from the property confiscated from the deportees.

Vendulka and her parents joined a queue at a long table where registration was carried out. Šimon and Karla had to fill out several forms, surrender the keys of their apartment, along with all family valuables, and pay outstanding payments for water and electricity. Then the German official told them where to sit. All around there lay piles of suitcases, and people jostled each other. The air reeked of urine. There were not enough toilets there, so people had to relieve themselves wherever they could. The hall was full of whispering, interrupted now and then by weeping, sobs, or coughing. The noise of the outside world could be heard from Veletržní Street just the other side of a wooden fence: people's footsteps and the sound of passing motor vehicles. The time spent waiting for the train's departure was punctuated only by the arrival of a vehicle belonging to the Jewish Community bringing food for the assembled crowd. But most of them were still eating the packed lunches they had brought with them for the journey. Vendulka's memory of the first night spent in the *Radiotrh* building was of a constant feeling of anxiety and apprehension, as well as the stench of urine, and the cold concrete floor. They spent two more days there before the Nazis herded them to the train.

They arrived at the station in a column of four. The column was accompanied by several German soldiers, who were joined at Bubny station by dog handlers. Vendulka and her parents knew they were headed for the concentration camp at Terezín (Theresienstadt). Some of their friends had already been sent there, as well as Karla's sister and Vendulka's cousin Miloš, who had lived just a few floors below at the same house in Lodecká Street. So they had basic, albeit vague, information. The train they boarded was formed of regular coaches with seats and windows that could be wound down and were not even blacked out. They were not yet the cattle trucks that the Nazis later used to transport the prisoners between the concentration camps. They realised that the cattle trucks might cause panic among those being transported and arouse concern among the non-Jewish inhabitants of Prague. Vendulka was cold after several sleepless nights, so Karla wrapped her in her coat and hugged her to her. The train shuddered and edged forward.

Packing essentials. (The Vogl family the evening before they left
for the transport, Prague, 1943, photo Jan Lukas)

Before the transport. (Vendulka before departure to concentration camp, Prague, 1943, photo Jan Lukas)

The last photograph together. (The Vogl family just before
the transport, Prague, 1943, photo Jan Lukas)

Terezín

"Hold onto me at all costs, whatever happens," Karla said and took her daughter firmly by the hand as the train arrived at Terezín. It was the morning of 8 March 1943. The train took them right into the town. By then the prisoners of the camp had built a branch line from nearby Bohušovice nad Ohří, so unlike the Jews on the previous transports, Vendulka and her parents didn't have to trudge two and a half kilometres on foot with their heavy luggage.

Soldiers herded them into a building known there as the *šlojska*, from the German word *Schleuse* meaning a lock on a river. There were lots of people everywhere pushing and shoving, and in this tense atmosphere the Nazis were barking orders. Their luggage and clothing was searched once more and any remaining valuables they had managed to hide were confiscated.

Šimon was placed in the men's block, while Karla and Vendulka were assigned to the Hamburg Barracks designated for the women. They each received a blanket and were ordered to go upstairs to the first floor. There they found a large room full of three-tiered bunks of unplaned wood, on which hundreds of women were sitting or lying. Most of them were emaciated, with sunken cheeks and circles under their eyes from exhaustion and lack of sleep. Vendulka would soon understand why. For supper she received dry bread with a little bit of margarine, and from the very first night she started to be tormented by fleas and bedbugs. She kept on scratching, but as soon as she eased the itch in one place, the troublesome insect would bite her somewhere else. To reach the toilet she had to weave her way carefully among the sleeping bodies. She silently observed what went on around her and listened to what the other women were saying. Some of them would describe their favourite foods, which they would like to taste again. Others recalled their lives before the war, and their voices would sometimes falter as they spoke about them. She didn't get much sleep. She hugged her mother and spent most of the night staring into the dark with eyes wide open.

During the following days she was acquainted with the camp regime. The Nazis had chosen a good site for their purposes. Most of the streets were at right-angles, so they had a good view of what went on in them. The town was surrounded by ramparts, which made the possibility of escape difficult. The ghetto considered of eleven large buildings within whose walls over forty thousand people were crowded onto plank beds. Thus the first general impression Vendulka had of Terezín was a dense concentration of human bodies, chaos, and the impossibility of intimacy, of being alone for a moment. Although they were allowed to move freely around the ghetto, the Jews were not allowed to walk on the pavement and the grassed areas, or loiter anywhere near the camp leadership building or the SS quarters.

The Terezín ghetto was under the command of the *SS Kommandantur*, while internal running of the ghetto was in the hands of the Jewish Council of Elders – the *Ältestenrat*, which was made up of several departments under the leadership of its Chairman. The leaders of the various departments were in charge of almost all activity in the ghetto, including administration, economic management, health, and cultural matters. The scope for self-government gave the impression that the Jews ran the town themselves, but the activity of the *Ältestenrat* was subordinate to the orders of the *SS Kommandantur*, the German camp administration.

Terezín served as a reception camp and transfer station prior to transfer to camps in Poland. Compared to the latter, conditions in Terezín were less stringent and intended to mask the mass murders, although even in those first days Vendulka and Karla repeatedly encountered men carrying dead bodies on stretchers. They cheered up a little when they discovered that Šimon was housed only a few blocks away, and that they were able to meet together for a short while in the evening after work for a chat. But their joy at seeing each other did not last long, however. After a couple of weeks Vendulka was transferred to house L 410, where girls between the ages of ten and seventeen were brought together. For the first time in her life she would be alone.

"You have to be strong. We'll see each other every evening," Karla reassured her. "Maybe it will be better for you there. You'll have more space and find some friends."

The house stood on the square right next to the church that was the dominant feature of the town. The house had thirty rooms, each of which housed between twenty and thirty girls of around fourteen years old. They were supervised by an adult woman whom they called the "*betreuerka*" (in some of the houses, particularly those with a strong Zionist leadership, the supervisor was known by the Hebrew word "*madricha*"), who helped Vendulka cope with the first days and nights, when her fear and anxiety prevented her from sleeping. In the middle of the room stood a stove and a wooden table surrounded by benches. There was no artificial light, so the inmates went to bed when it got dark. There was one shared bathroom on the ground floor, and sometimes Vendulka and her friends brought buckets of water up to their room. The water ran cold most of the time, even during the hardest frosts, and they had tepid water just once a week.

Food was what Vendulka found hardest to get used to. In the morning she was given black water vaguely resembling coffee, for lunch thin buckwheat or barley broth or a watery gravy with a few unpeeled potatoes, for supper dry bread, occasionally with a bit of margarine, and sometimes a spoonful of jam. But in time she even got used to that, and it turned out that her mother was right: in the new building she was better off than among the adult women. In fact she would know even enjoyment and fun when she managed to forget the ever-present walls, and the proximity of other bodies and death. She made friends with three girls of a similar age – Kitty, Dáša and Líza – and soon they formed an inseparable foursome. They volunteered together for work in the garden, where they occasionally managed to steal some fallen leaves or apples.

"Been scrumping again?" her mother would ask when they met, and they would tease each other about what delicacy they would prepare, or at least until they discovered for the first time what was called "a dose of Terezín", as severe diarrhoea was called in the ghetto.

When Vendulka wasn't working she would visit the so-called "*heim*", where Jewish teachers would give clandestine lessons. What pleased her most of all was meeting up with Fredy Hirsch, the leader at Hagibor in Prague, who had left for Terezín in December 1941. Thanks to his self-confident bearing and German origin, he had even earned a certain respect among a number of SS men, and as a result he managed to obtain space for a play area, and even "claim back" some individuals from planned eastbound transports.

In the early days of the ghetto all cultural expression was banned, but the Nazis soon realised that they could make use of prisoners' artistic activity to foster a false impression about the actual purpose of the Terezín ghetto, and create the legend of "The Führer Gives a City to the Jews", which was the title of a Nazi propaganda film produced in Terezín, starting in 1942. Cultural life gradually expanded to such an extent that it was hard for the Nazis to curb it. Prisoners included top-flight teachers, painters, artists and scientists of various nationalities, who, like Hirsch, sought to give their lives and the lives of their children some meaning at least.

Vendulka enjoyed most of all the lessons given by the painter and teacher Friedl Dicker-Brandeis, who came from Vienna. Before the war she had studied at the state Bauhaus in Weimar where her teachers had included famed artists such as Johannes Itten, Paul Klee and Wassily Kandinsky. She had emigrated to Czechoslovakia after Hitler's rise to power and was deported to the Terezín ghetto in 1942.

Her teaching method was based on a concept inspired by her studies at the Bauhaus. She perceived drawing as a path to self-knowledge, and the freeing of imagination and emotions. In fact, it was at the same time a form of therapy that enabled the children to cope better with the depressing everyday reality of the ghetto. Friedl encouraged Vendulka to draw the things she liked, so she drew her memories of nature or everyday life as she remembered it from outside the ghetto – the tall trees in the park, a car driving through an avenue of trees, studies of flowers and plants.

Friedl's professional guidance is evident in some of Vendulka's drawings, such as the use of perspective, which is not very common in the drawings of Vendulka's contemporaries, particularly in Terezín, where the drawings of otherwise talented children are inevitably influenced by trauma, which sometimes take the form of symptoms of regression to a certain kind of primitivism. (Šimon's influence was also significant, since he was very proficient at technical and architectural drawing, and Vendulka often drew with him.) Two of Vendulka's drawings also feature clothing creations that are very reminiscent of the style of illustrations in fashion magazines, which she would one day engage in professionally. Here too Friedl lent a guiding hand and patiently explained to her what she was doing wrong. She would encourage her to rethink her creations, and would sometimes actually get involved with the drawing herself. And so Vendulka made some more clothing sketches and imagined herself one day wearing one of her own creations.

Most of the children that Friedl Dicker-Brandeis taught in her lessons were later murdered by the Nazis, but before she herself died, their teacher managed to save almost five thousand of their drawings in two old suitcases. Ten of those drawings would become the property of Vendulka. They are now deposited in the Jewish Museum in Prague; four of the drawings are even double-sided because they had to save paper.

Paper was always in short supply in Terezín. Adults and children alike filled every available piece of paper with poems, notes and drawings that helped them forget for a moment the hunger, the Nazis' sadism, the uncertainty, and the threat of more transports. It is as if every one of their poems, notes, or drawings was not a work of art, but a magic spell that helped them break through the walls of the ghetto.

Drawing the world beyond the barbed wire... (Vendulka's drawing
from Terezín 1943, archive of the Jewish Museum, Prague)

...a world now beyond reach. (Vendulka's drawing from Terezín 1943, archive of the Jewish Museum, Prague)

She imagined herself one day wearing one of her own creations.
(Vendulka's drawing from Terezín 1943, archive of the Jewish
Museum, Prague)

"And would you believe that after a couple of months I got used to Terezín?" Vendulka said, raising her eyes to me. It looked as if she herself was surprised by the question. "Ever since I was small I was slightly frivolous by nature, and at the camp I quickly realised that I have to learn to centre my life on small things. To lose hope meant death. One of the things that raised my spirits every time were the letters from Honza Lukas. He wrote to me about what was happening at home in Prague and elsewhere in the republic, and he gave us a boost with his comforting words. I'm sure you'd like to see them..."

I nodded enthusiastically, but before I could reply, Vendulka added that she unfortunately lost them somewhere during the next transport.

"But that doesn't mean I was unaware of the grim things around me. I recall a little boy who was adopted by 'Aryan' parents before the war, and because he was a Jew he ended up in Terezín," she said, turning her head away again. But she continued in a firm voice: *"His mum and dad would make regular trips from Prague to visit him, and every time they said goodbye you could see how it broke their hearts. One morning he was found dead in the barracks. He died from hypothermia. That woman begged the guards to let her see him one more time to say goodbye, but they didn't let her. She collapsed on the ground, on that muddy, trampled courtyard. I can still hear her scream."*

I interrupted her to ask whether it wasn't time for another break and cup of tea, but Vendulka raised her palm in a gesture of reluctance. *"No, no, afterwards. I have to tell it all now."*

Since the summer of 1943 the prisoners of the Terezín had been observing some odd changes. The notices from the camp administration were now printed on artistically designed posters. The military designations of the streets were removed and they were given names. In the south-east corner of the square the prisoners were allowed to build a band stand where the local orchestra played promenade music. A café was established, even though the inhabitants of the ghetto could look inside only once in several months if they were in possession of a special ticket, and all they were served there was ersatz coffee. Shops started to appear in the ghetto filled with clothes, suitcases and footwear that the Nazis had confiscated from the inmates on their arrival. A playground, school and nursery were established for the children. Some of the regulations were also changed: the evening curfew was shifted from 8pm to 10pm and there were more areas accessible to the Jews. The alterations, which were part of the so-called "beautification operation", took place successively throughout the year until 23 June 1944, when its real purpose was revealed. That morning a car entered the camp containing three elegantly-dressed gentlemen. Their names were Frants Hvass, Eigil Juel Henningsen and Maurice Rossel. They were emissaries from the Danish Foreign Ministry, the Danish Red Cross, and the International Committee of the Red Cross. The car drove along a pre-ordained route, along which messengers were placed, who announced the arrival of the delegation. The delegation could then watch good-looking Jewish women unloading fresh vegetables from a van, someone scoring a goal in a football match, and finally a performance of the children's opera Brundibár. The audience applauded and the head of the delegation, Maurice Rossel from Switzerland, enthusiastically took photographs.

The three men received permission for their visit on the basis of a request from the Danish government to allow their representatives to visit 466 Danish Jews who were deported to Terezín in October 1943. They spent eight hours in the ghetto. The outcome was a tendentious report, of which Maurice Rossel was the main author. The ghetto was described as, by and large, a normal Jewish town, where conditions were comparable with those in the Protectorate, if not better. "The SS police gives the Jews the freedom to administer it themselves. The Terezín camp is a terminus camp, from which normally no one who has entered the ghetto is sent anywhere else." The Nazis' attempts to conceal the truth about Terezín had scored a victory.

And yet a month before the visit the Nazis had sent a transport of 7,500 Jewish prisoners to Auschwitz so that the ghetto should appear less overcrowded.

Like the other inmates, Karla and Šimon lived from the very first day in a state of anxiety about whether Terezín was a final destination. The words that put fear into everyone were "further east". No one had any specific information about what happened to Jews there, but no one returned from there, and after a while almost everyone fell silent.

One report did reach the ghetto, however. It was smuggled in by a Jewish prisoner who had managed to escape from the Auschwitz-Birkenau concentration camp. He described how thousands of Jews were disappearing into the gas chambers and crematoria. His name was Vítězslav Lederer. The Council of Elders either didn't believe him or were afraid to think about the implications of his report. "I personally conveyed to Dr Eppstein and Dr Baeck the report that Lederer brought us, and the chairman of the Council, Dr Eppstein, implored me not to divulge it, otherwise it could spell disaster for the almost 35 thousand inhabitants," Leo Holzer, who was head of the fire brigade in Terezín testified after the war. "We requested our friends to keep the secret, and were afraid of the consequences that would arise if this information reached the public in Terezín." For that reason, none of the other Jews in Terezín learned about the horrors that awaited them "in the East".

During the Vogls' period of imprisonment in Terezín, four transports left for Auschwitz. On 15 December 1943, a train left with 2,504 prisoners, followed three days later by another. On 15 May 1944 a transport left also with 2,504 Jewish inmates, and the following day a transport with 2,500 prisoners. A fifth was fixed for 18 May 1944, for a further 2,000 people, and Karla, Vendulka and Šimon Vogl were assigned to it. Just prior to the announcement, Vendulka was ill with tonsillitis, so that she had a headache, burning in her throat, and a high temperature. She heard her mother's words about the transport as if it was an echo in a mist.

"You must be strong and get better," Karla whispered in her ear, while stroking her hair. In that state of partial delirium Vendulka took a coloured pencil and started to draw a picture on the ceiling above her head. It could have been of a park in Karlovy Vary, the balcony in Lodecká Street, her pals from Hagibor, or the children's house at Terezín. The drawing grew into a largish fresco. Her arm hurt, but something impelled her, a feeling that she mustn't give up. She finished the drawing a few days before the departure.

Auschwitz

This time they were cattle trucks. A hundred prisoners were squeezed into each of them. They could each take a small piece of luggage, and before the soldiers slammed the doors behind them, they placed a bucket of water inside along with several loaves of bread. It was dark in the wagon, and there was so little room that it was almost impossible to lie down. The prisoners relieved themselves in a chamber pot that was handed round and then emptied out of the barred window. Vendulka couldn't tell how long they were travelling. Time ceased to exist for her. Thirst was the worst thing. The bucket of water was soon empty. The train made frequent stops, but they were not allowed out of the wagon. A hose with water was stuck through the bars and they tried to catch the water in the bucket, or in their mouths, and catch every last drop on their tongues and faces.

The journey took two days and two nights, or maybe only one night. Vendulka fell into a strange state of apathy in which she ceased to be aware of time, space, people, and the stench. It seemed to her like when she was little and submerged her head under the surface of the bath water, so that she heard how the sounds of the outside world were transformed into dull, muffled notes that were interrupted only by the popping of the soap bubbles as they burst.

Transport Eb came to its final stop at Auschwitz on 23 May 1944.

"Raus! Raus! Get out!" Vendulka was roused from her apathy by the fierce orders of the SS and the barking of dogs. Anyone who was too slow received a blow across the back from a rifle butt or a stick. They had to climb quickly onto the backs of lorries that drove them to the concentration camp. "High voltage", Vendulka read on the signs fixed to the barbed wire.

Most of the transports had to undergo selection as soon as they arrived. The Nazis then sent the weak, old and ill people straight to the gas chambers. The rest had their heads shaved and were separated into men's and women's blocks. But the transport on which Vendulka and her parents arrived was treated differently. There was no initial selection, they could even keep the luggage they had brought from Terezín, and their heads were not shaved. They were herded along with the other prisoners into a huge room in some former stables, where they spent the night on plank beds. In the morning the guards started to drive them out in turn to have a number tattooed on their right forearms – slightly higher than usual in the case of Vendulka and Karla as the tattooist was distracted and in a hurry. Šimon then had to go with the other men to another building, but they were relieved to discover that they could associate with each other as in Terezín. The camp they were taken to – Auschwitz-Birkenau, *Bauabschnitt* (construction segment) IIb – occupied an area roughly equivalent to 15 football pitches. It was adjacent to the so-called gypsy camp BIIe and consisted of several rows of long wooden huts. They lacked windows and simply had air vents below the roof. Like in Terezín the inmates had to squeeze onto unplaned planks that stretched along the left and right walls of the hut. Each side was partitioned to create three-tier sleeping platforms with six prisoners on each tier, making a total of eighteen prisoners in each compartment. There were stoves at each end of the huts which were lit only when it was very cold; a brick smoke flue ran along the floor from one stove to the other. In the middle there was a low brick wall where everything important happened. It was where clothes and blankets were laid out and dried, where food was shared out, and orders were given.

Each block was under the command of a kapo from the ranks of the Jewish prisoners. From the first moment the kapos struck fear into Vendulka. She had known some of them from Terezín as kind and decent people, but here they were transformed into sadistic stooges of the Nazi guards. Anyone who was late for *appell* (roll call), who stood differently from the rest, who managed to get a little extra food, who forgot to salute an SS man, or who laughed, was immediately beaten and kicked by the kapo. The kapos knew that the slightest slip-up would mean demotion to the status of ordinary prisoner.

Vendulka and her parents discovered on the first day how privileged the members of the last transport from Terezín were compared to others in Auschwitz. Not only were families able to be together, but the children continued to be cared for by assistants under the leadership of Fredy Hirsch. However, by the time Vendulka arrived in the camp he was already dead. Fellow prisoners planning an uprising in the camp had asked him to lead it. Since he was widely respected and people trusted him, the representatives of the resistance movement thought that he was the only person the prisoners would follow if he called on them to rise up. The last person to talk to him was a young Slovak Jew, Rudolf Vrba, who managed to escape from Auschwitz and write a report that would convince the international community about what was happening behind the electrified barbed wire.

I gazed across the room at this strong young German, at his open, enquiring face and I knew that he was a man who would follow his conscience. I repeated to him the message from Schmulewski [the leader of the resistance movement]. His expression did not change. He remained silent. Two minutes later I said, "Fredy, you're the only man who can do it. The only man they'll follow." "But Rudi," he said in something like a whisper, "what about the children? 'This was the moment I had feared. I knew how much he loved those kids, how much they loved him. He was their second father, the axis on which the young lives turned. "Fredy," I said, "the children are going to die. That you must believe. But tens of thousands of children have died here before and now we have a chance to put a stop to it. To smash the camp so that no other kids will ever be gassed here. Think of it that way... A few hundred die today because nobody can save them. But tens of thousands of other youngsters will live."

His face was pale and tense; his hand shook as he lit a cigarette.

After the conversation with Vrba on 8 March 1944, Hirsch asked for an hour to think it over. Shortly afterwards, the man who was expected to lead the uprising died from an overdose of barbiturates. Mystery still surrounds the death of Fredy Hirsch. Some say that he deliberately took the overdose, others that it was a murder organised by the doctors of the family camp, who were afraid of the planned uprising and therefore killed Fredy to avert it. What is known for sure is that he was carried off – either already dead or dying – to the gas chamber with the rest.

Vendulka heard about what happened the following day from her friends from the previous transports. At the beginning of March 1944, about 3,800 people remained in the family camp out of the 5,007 deported in the September 1943 transport from Terezín. The remainder had died from undernourishment, illness, or accidents, or they were murdered. In their documents were written the letters "SB", which stood for "*Sonderbehandlung*", meaning "special treatment" – for six months they were placed in protective quarantine. That period expired precisely on 8 March. At roll call that day the kapos informed the prisoners of family camp BIIb that they would be transferred to the Heydebreck labour camp. No such camp existed, but the prisoners were unaware of that. The obediently boarded the waiting lorries, which immediately took them on the planned route to the Auschwitz gas chambers. Their final moments were described by Rudolf Vrba:

> The lorries began to snarl again and move towards the gate like an armoured division. The noise of the engines seem to fill the camp, to drown my ears. Then, suddenly, over this harsh, imperative note, I heard a new, sweet sound. The sound of a thousand women singing. And the song was the Czechoslovak National Anthem – "Where is my home?" It faded away as the lorry disappeared. New voices took over with a new song, inspired by the same thought. This time it was the Jewish National Anthem – Hatikvah. Hope. For hours, I stood outside that barracks, long after the last lorry had gone and the stench of exhaust had disappeared. I stood there, tortured, until I saw dark smoke mix with the huge yellow flame that rose from the crematorium.

Vendulka's friends at that time in the camp, who had witnessed the March events, included Dita Krausová, her friend from Hagibor, with whom she played volleyball, and with whom, before the Protectorate was declared, she had had portraits taken at the photographic studio on Na Příkopě street. Dita had slept through that fateful night and woke next morning to find the camp suddenly half-empty. The remaining prisoners moved around the deserted camp like shadows. In one of the barracks she saw some thick blankets lying on a plank bed, so she took one. She realised that it had been left by one of the men who had just been murdered, but the conditions in the camp had ridden her of sensitivity and compassion. She had a blanket. She had a lovely thick blanket at last.

The reasons why family camp BIIb was set up are still unknown. It might have been part of a plan to conceal the extermination of the Jews from the outside world, like in Terezín. But what had been possible to stage manage after a year-long preparation in the Terezín ghetto was unthinkable in a place where the crematoria were visible from everywhere, and where people looked like skeletons covered in skin. Maybe it was just a frightful Nazi ideological cocktail of thoroughness, irrationality and sadism.

When Vendulka found out how the Jews from the September and subsequent transports had died, and that Fredy Hirsch had probably committed suicide, she realised that the same fate now awaited her and her parents. She turned her face towards the crematorium from which smoke was rising. At night flames shot out of the chimney and the air was full of a sweet stench.

In spite of the "privileges" conferred on them by the letters "SB" in the camp identity papers, conditions there were dreadful. Whenever someone tried to escape, they would be caught and killed by the Nazis, who would force the prisoners to look at the corpse. They would be made to stand for hours on end on the *Appellplatz* without water in the blazing sun. Vendulka no longer noticed the bed bugs, fleas and scabies; diarrhoea was what troubled her most. The food there was much poorer than in Terezín. They received nothing on rising and just ersatz coffee during the morning. The first meal was around mid-day, mostly a little soup. She was constantly hungry and felt increasing exhaustion. People would creep past her wearily, transformed into shadows. The old and sick soon died.

Scarcely a month had passed since their arrival and the Nazis announced a new selection. Chaos erupted in the camp. People feared the same fate as the prisoners from the previous transports. Vendulka went to the selection, followed immediately by Karla. They had to strip naked and walk past a number of SS men sitting at table. Vendulka felt ashamed, and the inspection seemed interminably long. But she knew she had to look self-confident and pretend to be older and more adult. The selection took women from the age of fifteen, but she was only thirteen, so she had to lie about her age. It saved her life. The commission deemed her capable of work. Shortly afterwards her father also underwent a selection in another part of the camp.

None of the prisoners knew whether it was a ruse intended to get them to the gas chambers without resistance. Nevertheless Vendulka's parents tried to reassure her.

"The worst is behind us, things will be better now." But dark thoughts continued to run through her mind.

Šimon was the first to hear about the departure date. They assigned him to another part of the camp, so he came to say goodbye to Vendulka through the barbed-wire fence. They could not touch each other, but stood facing each other with tears pouring down their faces. What Šimon told his only daughter that time Vendulka would disclose to no one. It would remain her secret for ever.

Then Šimon Vogl lined up with the other men in a column of four and they passed the Auschwitz crematorium on the way to the departure platform. Some of them mimed wheels turning as a sign that they were really boarding a train to leave Auschwitz. It was the last time Vendulka saw her father.

The women who underwent the selection were taken by the Nazis to hut number twenty-five and herded into the showers. Some of the women started to scream in anxiety and bang on the locked door. Karla held Vendulka's hand tightly in hers as at other difficult moments, and hugged her to her. Then hot water began to run from the showers and the room filled with steam. They both gave enormous sighs of relief. Someone started to pray and thank God for surviving.

The shower was followed by a further inspection. The Nazis checked to see if any of the women had something under their clothes. They would hide photos of their loved ones in their hair, or under their tongues. Anyone found with contraband was beaten. Finally they were all led outside, where the footwear and clothes they had removed had been piled up. Vendulka couldn't find her own shoes, so she quickly reached for another pair of a similar size. Afterwards they had to line up again naked in double file and the Nazis handed out clothes to them.

Vendulka and Karla left the camp just a few days before it was liquidated. That day something odd occurred. Suddenly the crematoria stopped smoking and helium balloons rose above Auschwitz. The scene seemed to Vendulka to be from another world, like something out of a Jules Verne novel, or posters for the 1891 Jubilee World Fair with a photograph of the Kysibelka balloon that offered aerial trips over the exhibition site. Jan Lukas had once shown her the picture. The Nazis had a different purpose for them, of course. The balloons were anchored above the concentration camp as air-raid protection. Allied aircraft were increasingly carrying out bombing raids of Poland in the summer of 1944 from bases in partially liberated Italy, and the balloons were supposed to stop them flying over. It happened to be 6 June 1944 – "D Day", the allied invasion of the Normandy beaches.

The family camp was liquidated shortly afterwards. In the course of three nights, from 10 to 12 July 1944 the Nazis sent the 6,500 men, women and children who had managed to survive to the gas chambers.

The Protectorate

The news that Jan Lukas received from Vendulka and her parents was vague because of Nazi censorship. He sent them several letters and parcels to Terezín, but received only terse replies, saying they were well looked after, they had enough food, and a roof over their heads... He had his doubts about whether this was true, but at least he could be sure they were still alive. In autumn 1944 he opened at breakfast a letter postmarked Christianstadt, Germany. Karla and Vendulka wrote to him that they had left Auschwitz and had been sent on a transport to a labour camp. They needed toothbrushes and winter clothes. They had no news of Šimon. He had been sent to another place, probably another labour camp. Jan left his breakfast unfinished, took off the sweater he was wearing, gathered a few other items from his flat, and set off for the nearest shop. He sent the parcel that very day. In doing so he saved Vendulka's life, but he wouldn't find that out until the war was over.

He himself tried by whatever means to survive in the conditions of the Protectorate. He continued to travel all over the country, but the subject-matter of the photography changed. Social and political commitment gave way to non-adversarial photographs of everyday life: women exercising, portraits of the artist Jiří Brdečka at work and of the actress Adina Mandlová, as well as photographs of theatrical productions, or scenes from a girls' camp at Medlov Pond with an accompanying text by the writer Ladislav Matějka:

To lie in the grass on a slope where there is plenty of southern sun to ripen the wild strawberries, to lie in a bed of thyme like a bucolic shepherd and whistle at the marching clouds. To sing all your cares and pains and send them beyond the clouds far from you.

The reason for the change was not just fear, but the simple fact that there was no interest in any other kind of photography, and Jan Lukas needed to earn a living somehow. This was also reflected in the later books of his photographs in which he included almost no photos from that period, even though he continued to publish diligently – mostly in the magazines *Eva, Pramen* and *Milena*. His photos reflect the paradox of those days. Whereas in Terezín, Auschwitz and other camps, Czech Jews and Romanies, as well as German and Czech anti-fascists were dying every day, people in the Protectorate still lived apparently ordinary lives. The turmoil of the war was far away: football matches between Sparta and Slavie took place at the Letná stadium, and the people of Prague could visit any of the city's 80 cinemas and attend premieres of new films with favourite comedians. Oldřich Nový courted beautiful women in the film *Christian* (1939), Vlasta Burian played a fare-dodger who became a Station Master in the film of the same name (1941) and Jindřich Plachta tames his shrewish wife *Philomena in The Five Squirrels* (1944). Those who stayed at home could enjoy an evening concert on the radio, possibly featuring Jan Seidel's 1st symphony "Prologue".

In short, it was a life of entertainment, everyday worries and illusions amidst the horrors of war. Even the Nazis regarded Prague as a safe city – safer than those in Germany. They moved a lot of their important institutions and companies there. The *Kinderlandverschickung* organisation, for instance, which arranged accommodation and holiday camps for German children made homeless in bombed German towns, set up several branches in Prague. The atmosphere and political situation radically changed after the assassination of the Nazi *Reichsprotektor* Reinhard Heydrich on 27 May 1942, when Lidice and Ležáky were annihilated and hundreds of Czech resistance members and their families were murdered at the Kobylisy firing range or in concentration camps. But Czech territory was never in the front line of battle. People went on listening to the fox-trot, and spending time at the swimming pool, or on dates in the gardens on Petřín Hill.

Indeed Jan Lukas used to take walks there too. While photographing performances at the Švanda Theatre near Újezd he fell under the spell of the actress and dancer Milena Nocarová. She stepped into his viewfinder and soon after into his life. She spent weekends with him and friends at Medlov near Olomouc – on one of those occasions Jan Lukas took stock shots at the local pond for the *Eva* magazine mentioned earlier – and they would also go to cafés and cinemas in Prague together.

Their relationship was boosted by an illness that confined Jan to bed at the end of 1944 and almost caused his death. He neglected an attack of tonsillitis and the infection penetrated deeper into his system resulting in a severe bone-marrow inflammation. Purulent swellings appeared all over his body, which had to be surgically lanced and cleaned. They were particularly troublesome on his hips and knees, causing him to limp, as he could not bend his leg. As he avoided bending the leg to avoid the pain his tendons shortened to such a degree that the doctors had to stretch the limb artificially. Eventually he had to be hospitalised in Pardubice. He remained there with Milena until the end of the war, and she visited him regularly. When the allies carried out a bombing raid on the city, the hospital staff rapidly made for the air-raid shelter, while he was left helpless in bed expecting a stray bomb to land on his ward.

Nobody wished us a safe return. (Prague people at the time
of the Jewish transports, no date, photo Jan Lukas)

The pace of life in the Protectorate. (Moravia, 1940, photo Jan Lukas)

Bewitched. (Wedding photo of Jan Lukas's bride Milena Nocarová.
1946, photo Jan Lukas)

Christianstadt

For the journey from Auschwitz they were given a piece of bread and a little piece of margarine. It was summer and humid, and in the unventilated cattle truck the fat soon melted and became a smelly, greasy liquid. Vendulka had already learned never to eat food all at once, because it would be a long time before they would get any more. So she just nibbled the bread. It took a whole day for the train to reach Christianstadt, a subcamp of the Gross-Rosen concentration camp in Western Poland. As soon as Vendulka and Karla climbed down from the cattle truck they instinctively lifted their gaze to the horizon in search of smoking chimneys and crematoria, but there were none. And there was no omnipresent sweet stench like in Auschwitz. They were surprised to see that it was a women's camp. Even the guards were nearly all women, most of them around twenty or thirty years old. When the prisoners were lined up they were told emphatically that they could expect a tough life and rough work; there was a high mortality rate and only those who worked hard and obeyed the rules would survive. They were then sent to their huts.

In Auschwitz Vendulka had already learnt the basic rules of survival: merge into the crowd, don't stand out in any way, always be neatly turned out, don't smile unnecessarily, don't talk aloud with anyone, and be on time for the roll call. The roll calls were early in the morning, frequently at four or five a.m. At the first of them, representatives of the German explosives works Dynamit AG were present. They walked along the two rows of women and selected those who looked healthiest and strongest, including Karla and Vendulka. Luckily they had only spent a month at Auschwitz and managed to avoid typhus, dysentery and the guards' truncheons, so they didn't look as wretched as the others.

They spent the first weeks in the explosives factory. It consisted of a number of concrete buildings erected in the middle of pine woods so as not to be visible to allied bombers. The prisoners carried containers of potassium and sodium nitrate, the basic components of dynamite, and poured them into cartridge cases. The chemicals ate away their skin and their hair turned reddish-brown due to the effects of the compound. When Vendulka glanced at Karla during one work break she almost didn't recognise her mother.

After a few weeks, the Nazis separated them. Vendulka remained in the dynamite factory, but Karla was transferred to work in the forest for the Siemens Bau Union company. She felled trees with the other prisoners. They had to cut off all the branches and carefully strip the trunks. In the new gap between the trees they built a road to a new Siemens factory. Karla would come back to the camp exhausted. On the bunk bed in the evening she would tell Vendulka about how a lorry would bring enormous rocks to where they were, and pile them up. Then they had to break them up into chippings with sledgehammers. Many of the women injured themselves in the process, and a few of them were blinded when splinters of the stone pierced their retinas.

Karla had to walk several hours to work and make the same journey back to camp in the late afternoon. Although a train ran to the Siemens works for the employees, the Jews were not allowed to use it. When they were building the road they were supervised by foremen from among the Germans. Karla told Vendulka that they were fortunately not as brutal and dangerous as the camp guards, and they never beat the prisoners,

Some of them could even be persuaded to send a letter or receive a parcel on behalf of a prisoner. Not all the parcels arrived, but if they did, the prisoners were obliged to give the foremen a bribe. In that way Karla managed to send a letter to Jan Lukas, who sent them among other things toothbrushes and a thick sweater. It was just in time: the winter of 1944 at Christianstadt was harsh and temperatures dropped well below zero. The wooden huts were draughty and there was nothing to heat them with.

The hope that the war would soon be over boosted their morale. Allied air raids became more frequent, and air-raid alarms were regularly sounded in the labour camp. For the first time it occurred to them that if the aircraft attacked their camp they could try to escape in the ensuing chaos. Although the bombers ignored their camp, Karla wanted to be prepared. As winter approached they were issued with coats, with a rectangle of striped prison cloth sewn onto the back of them. At night Karla unstitched the cloth and hid beneath it a patch of the same colour as the coat. So outwardly she and Vendulka wore the sign that identified them, but under it there was a piece of clean cloth in the event of a future escape. They simply had to cover the rectangle on the prison coat.

Meanwhile the Nazis transferred Karla back to the dynamite factory where she was with Vendulka. They were able to be together but they were in a new department where the work was more dangerous. They had to pour the explosive mixture into detonators. Injuries were frequent. The chemical compound burned the skin and caused infections and inflammation, and as they had no right to penicillin, the prisoners often died of blood poisoning. They also worked through the night as the need for explosives grew, now that the German army was suffering more losses on the eastern and western fronts. Karla and Vendulka would take the shifts in turns and sleep just a few hours a day. When they were not working with the explosive they had to dig sand in the local gravel-pit for the construction of new roads.

The days wore on, during which they filled detonators or worked with sledgehammers and pickaxes, until 27 February 1945. That morning there was a snap roll call at Christianstadt. Vendulka and Karla leaped out of their beds and moments later were standing to attention in line. It must have been around three or four in the morning with no sign yet of daybreak in the east. The guards repeatedly called the roll for a recount and then sent the prisoners back to the huts to pack only the necessities. Vendulka put on several layers of clothes. Lukas's sweater kept her warm under her coat. The first glimmer of daylight could now be seen and the sky was clear. The hunched and shrouded figures in a column of four were accompanied by armed soldiers. Some rode bicycles, while others walked alongside the column with dogs. The Christianstadt prisoners were setting off on a death march.

Death March

The death march was one of the methods of murder perfected by the Nazis. The primary aim of the death marches was to clear the concentration, labour and prisoner-of-war camps as the German troops retreated. In spite of increasing defeats, the Nazis were unwilling to abandon their delusional ideas about racial purity and a "final solution to the Jewish problem", so the death marches were used for the targeted murder of prisoners, who were made to march for weeks without food, water or rest. Those who collapsed from exhaustion were shot in the back of the neck. Anyone who tried to escape was shot to death or torn to pieces by dogs. The corpses were loaded onto horse carts or remained lying by the roadside. Only a tenth of the prisoners at most survived the marches.

They walked in silence. Vendulka was aware only of the rhythmical tramp of worn-out footwear, and the moving heels of those marching wearily ahead of her. Once more time disappeared. She submerged herself beneath the indifferent surface of her consciousness in order not to hear the occasional rifle-butt blows, rifle shots, and barking of orders. In her head she repeated over and over again, almost manically, the words: "Keep going. Don't give up." They by-passed villages and towns. They slept out in the open, leaning against each other or lying side by side like teaspoons in a kitchen drawer.

"We'll make a run for it," Karla whispered to Vendulka one night before they went to sleep. "There are too many of us for them to keep watch on us all. We'll wait for when they change guard and go to the village for supplies."

A few days later they joined up with another death march from a different subcamp of the Gross-Rosen concentration camp. To her enormous surprise Karla noticed among the hunched figures Věra and Hana, daughters of close friends of her grandparents. Before the war they had lived at Velim in Central Bohemia, where their father Rudolf Glaser owned a well-known chocolate and chewing-gum factory. They wanted to give each other a hug of welcome, but the guards forcibly separated them, so they just quietly shared the news of what had happened to them. The cousins' brother had escaped to Great Britain and was serving in the RAF, and their parents had died in the Lodz ghetto, where their family was transported to in 1941. The cousins had survived Terezín and Auschwitz before ending up on the death march. Karla told them about her escape plan, but they refused to join her.

"The war is ending, Karla, there is no sense in taking the risk," Věra argued. "They'll shoot you before you manage to hide. And if you do manage to escape, where will you go? They'll report you in the first village you go through."

But Karla and Vendulka were unwilling to abandon their plan.

"What do you think will happen to us in the end? Do you really believe the Germans will just let us go?" Karla replied, not giving way.

After several more days they reached the edge of a burnt-out village. All that remained were a few barns, and charred chimneys that stuck up like fingers out of the ruins of the houses. Beyond the remains of the gardens were fields that were once cultivated, and beyond them could be seen the dark outline of a forest. It was overcast and there was no light from either stars or the moon. Some of the guards set about lighting a fire while the others went to find somewhere to sleep in the barns and sheds.

"We'll do it today," Karla whispered to Vendulka. They didn't go to sleep that night. They waited until the others were nodding off and started cautiously to creep away. Once they were out of the firelight and out of sight of the guards, they got up and ran crouched across the field to the forest. They stretched their arms out in front of them to stop the branches slashing their faces, and groped their way through the trees deeper into the forest. When they stopped exhausted in order to take a rest, they held their breath for a few moments and listened out for the sound of the guards' voices and their dogs. But they heard nothing. All around them was darkness and silence. They were alone.

After such a long run they needed to rest and lay down beneath the branches of fallen trees. They covered the branches with a layer of moss to protect themselves at least slightly from the frost. Karla put her arms round Vendulka and hugged her to her. They were cold, tired and hungry, but were finally free after many months.

In the morning they set off again, numb with cold. But as they were now free of the guards' surveillance they could go where they wanted. They had no idea where they were, but sensed that they should head south. After a few hours they reached a small-ish town. To enter it meant risking detection, but they couldn't hide in the forest, and they had to eat. Karla covered the prisoner symbol on their coats with a patch and they set off among the houses. They now looked like war refugees who had been made homeless and were seeking shelter. In the first street, however, they were stopped by a three-member Hitlerjugend patrol. Karla stood in front of Vendulka determined to protect her and fight. The young Germans ordered them to roll up their sleeves. Karla wanted to take advantage of the fact that their concentration camp numbers were tattooed slightly higher than usual, but one of the members of the Nazi patrol dashed over to her and pulled the sleeve right up to the elbow. Without further questions the youths arrested them and led them off to the small local jail. Two Polish women, who had also tried to escape, were already there. The four of them spent another night there without food or water.

They were awoken by the sound of a key in the lock. A German in civilian clothes stood in the doorway. He told them to get up and come with him.

"Are you going to shoot us?" Karla asked him.

"You'll go to the camp at Weisswasser," the man replied without looking at her.

Karla did not believe him. When they left the jail she looked around her expecting to see a firing squad. But there was no one there. She and Vendulka and the two Poles were indeed loaded onto a lorry and taken to a concentration camp. It was full of Hungarian Jewish women, and they were given a medical inspection on arrival by a French doctor.

They stayed there three days before setting off once more on a death march. As on the previous one, they were accompanied by

German soldiers on bicycles and with dogs. It was freezing. The soldiers constantly urged the prisoners on and it became increasingly clear to Karla that they would not last long at such a fast pace. What would then happen to them she witnessed several times a day. The muzzle of pistol placed on the back of the neck and a shot. She therefore kept scanning the landscape surreptitiously, seeking an opportune moment for them to attempt an escape. That moment arrived when they were going round some sharp bends in a road surrounding by thick forest. She looked in front of her and then behind, and just when the guards in front disappeared round a bend and the ones behind had not yet appeared from around the previous bend, she grasped Vendulka firmly by the hand and hissed "Now!" as she pulled her out of the road. They ran deeper into the forest and hid behind a tree. They closed their eyes, trying to control their breathing, silently praying that the guards hadn't noticed anything and the procession would keep advancing. After seemingly endless minutes the sound of footsteps faded and silence once more descended on the forest. They had managed to escape a death march for the second time. They were alone once more. Moreover they each had two potatoes in their pockets that they had been issued with at Weisswasser and hidden for when they would have greater need of them.

They once more headed south, not stopping until their reached the streets of the first town. They walked through them anxiously, fearing that some patrol might again stop them. But no one took any notice of them. People passed them by without looking at them. The moment that they lost their fear and stopped surreptitiously glancing at every passer-by, sirens sounded. An air raid warning. Within a few minutes the streets were empty. Karla and Vendulka dashed to the nearest house and asked a number of women who had run there for shelter whether they could shelter with them. They survived the raid huddled together and with their heads bowed. When the "all clear" siren sounded they quickly left the shelter and the town. They didn't stop until they reached a nearby farm, where Karla asked for food and water. The farmer evidently suspected what they were, but didn't comment on their request. He went into the house and returned with a cup of water, a piece of bread, and some cheese.

Fortified, they set off for the next town, where Karla managed to exchange two gold fillings, which had loosened from her teeth during the death march, for some money. She was clenching that unexpected treasure in her hand when a lorry with Wehrmacht soldiers passed them. She raised her hand and waved at them. Vendulka stared at her in amazement, mystified by her mother's action. But Karla confidently asked the soldiers if they happened to be heading for the rail station, and whether they could give them a lift. As soon as they were seated in the back of the truck, Vendulka turned to her and asked her what she was doing for God's sake. How could she know they wouldn't realise what they were.

"What if they put us up against a wall somewhere and shoot us? she whispered fearfully.

"They won't," Karla reassured her. "They've been at the front and they know as well as we do that the war is coming to an end. They've already had their fill of killing."

They boarded a train with forged papers. Vendulka had no idea how her mother had come by them. Maybe she had already obtained them in the concentration camp and hidden them in a seam, or she had got hold of them at the last moment. In all events the papers saved their lives. The wheels of the railway coach gave a screech and the train started moving. After two long years spent in concentration and labour camps, and on death marches, they were heading for home.

They still had a long journey ahead of them. They had to change trains several times, and then an orange glow appeared on the horizon ahead – Dresden was ablaze after the bombing. They spent three days on the city outskirts while the worst of the fires were being put out. They continued their journey through Sudetenland and then into the heart of Czech territory, until at last they saw the silhouette of Prague from the train window and their eyes welled up with tears. They quickly wiped their eyes and choked back their tears. The war wasn't over yet and they were still in danger.

Back Home

"The Prague we returned to was a completely different city from the one we had left two years before. I don't know what I imagined," Vendulka said as she raised her eyes to me. The tea I was holding in my hand had long gone cold, and I had scarcely taken a sip from it.

"You see most of my relatives and friends had ended up in concentration camps and we had no idea where to go. My mother, who had been extremely courageous the whole time, suddenly became frightened that someone would recognise us and report us. Or we'd be caught when they checked our papers. She wanted us to spend the night hidden under the train platform, but I persuaded her to call her best friend. I was terribly hungry and cold, and I was tired. I don't remember any more where that lady lived or where we went. I only remember that she ran a hot bath for us. I shut my eyes and wished that moment would last for ever. She gave us clean clothes. I was given some of her daughter's clothes and we finally had a good meal after so long. But my mother started to be paranoid and feared that if the Germans found us they would murder her friend's entire family. She kept repeating that she couldn't have it on her conscience, so in the end we left."

"Did you contact Jan Lukas? Didn't you try to ask for his help? I was curious to know.

"Of course," Vendulka nodded. "Mother and I called at their place on Mělnická Street, but they told us he was in hospital in Pardubice."

"So where did you go?" I asked impatiently.

"To some other friends whose name I've also forgotten, I'm afraid. But I do remember that my mother was so weak that I had to support her. We were warmly received, but after the first night the same situation repeated itself. Mother started to be afraid that

those people she loved were at risk. I expect you'll find it hard to believe, but she said on that occasion that the best thing would be for us to return to Terezín. She kept repeating that it couldn't be long, and someone in Terezín would help us hide. She even managed to contact some people in the camp, but they firmly recommended us not to try to go there. Instead they told us to give ourselves up to some Czech police officers, and ask then to put us in prison, as it could save our lives to spend our time in a cell until the end of the war."

"And you seriously considered that?" I asked in surprise.

"Yes, Mum wanted to do it, but I screamed at her that I wasn't going into any more prisons. I became completely hysterical at the thought of it," Vendulka told me disconcertedly. "On the spur of the moment I ran away from my mother and wandered around the city. While she was desperately looking for me I remembered my aunt Fany, who lived at Sadská near Nymburk. I had a bit of money that some of the friends had given me, so I bought a ticket and caught a train."

Vendulka sat down in a compartment alongside an elderly man who was travelling with his grand-daughter. She guessed that she and the girl were about the same age. When she looked at her she realised she had no papers. She started to panic. If the police arrived they would immediately arrest her. Just as the thought occurred to her, she heard voices from the next compartment.

"Good morning. Your identity papers."

She turned to her fellow passenger with a look of desperation. She blurted out to them that she had forgotten her identity card in Prague and didn't know what to do. Before the man had time to react, the police were standing in the doorway. Vendulka would never know whether her fellow passenger believed her lie, or whether he realised that she was fleeing the Nazis. In all events, he put on a show for the police, convincing them that both girls were his grand-daughters, who were travelling with him to the country, and he had stupidly left their identity cards at home. When the train arrived at Sadská, Vendulka thanked the man and quickly made her way to her aunt's.

Fany Blabolová had a pharmacy in Sadská. She was strong-willed lady with a very high voice, and Vendulka recalled from her pre-war visits that she was an excellent cook. As soon as Fany set eyes on her, the colour drained from her aunt's face and she gaped at her open-mouthed for a good few seconds. She had given up hope that Vendulka or her parents were alive, and now here was her niece in front of her. She hugged her tightly and tears sprang to their eyes.

Over a bowl of hot soup Vendulka explained to her the situation they were in, and how she and her mother had quarrelled. At that moment her aunt's strong will came to the fore. She called to her son to get in the car straight away and drive to Prague for Karla. A few hours later they were happily greeting each other in the doorway. Fany told Karla in no uncertain terms that there was no way she was prepared to discuss the danger of hiding them.

"The best thing will be to act normally," she told Karla. "Quite simply, some relatives from Prague are paying me a visit."

She would talk about them to her neighbours as "a battle-axe from Prague and her little kid who needs some fresh country air after a long illness." They hid at the aunt's until 8 May 1945, when the war ended. It happened to be Karla's forty-second birthday. They could return home at last. A German officer's family, which had moved into their apartment on Lodecká Street, had now been moved out. That family returned to Germany by train from Bubny station, from which Vendulka and her parents had left for Terezín two years before.

The wheels of history had moved on a notch and clicked back into place.

Vendulka was glad to be able to sleep in her own bed in her own bedroom that evening. She was happy that she and her mother had managed to survive in the end, but she was missing her father, whose absence made the apartment painfully silent.

It is not clear what happened to Šimon Vogl after he boarded the lorry at Auschwitz. According to available information in the archive, he was taken to the Gross-Rosen concentration camp, where he worked in a stone mine. So he was only about twenty kilometres from Karla and Vendulka, although they knew nothing about each other's presence. The working conditions in the camp were particularly cruel, and it is estimated that a third of the 125,000 prisoners died.

The Nazis started to clear the camp at the end of January 1945. In February, six thousand prisoners were dispatched from there on a death march. They included Šimon Vogl. Some of them boarded open coal trucks, and many of them froze to death on the way. The train passed through Dresden and Leipzig on the way to the Buchenwald concentration camp. The commander of the concentration camp did not allow the train to go through Linz, so it headed for the Mauthausen concentration camp. The remaining prisoners set off on a march through the territory of the protectorate – Gross-Rosen was located just sixty kilometres from the Czech border. One hundred and seventy nine prisoners who were weak and incapable of continuing were brutally murdered near Choustníkovo Hradiště. After the war their remains were found in several mass graves, but it was impossible to identify them.

In the first weeks after the war Karla and Vendulka still hoped that Šimon had survived. They believed that he was simply unable to get home, and that they would eventually see him again. Karla explained to her daughter that such things happened after World War I: men returned from the front sometimes many months after their relatives were already mourning them. Karla and Vendulka's last hopes were dashed when the phone rang and an unknown man was heard at the other end. He told them he had been on a death march with Šimon Vogl, and was there at the moment when he died. They agreed that the man would come at one o'clock the next day and tell them all about it. Then he hung up.

Karla and Vendulka waited impatiently, but nobody came. Finally, later that evening, Šimon's cousin Miloš Vogl, who lived two floors below them, paid them a call. He was one of the few relatives who had managed to survive concentration camp and return home. With a trembling voice he told them he had received a surprise visit. The man who telephoned them yesterday had rung his doorbell by mistake. Miloš regretted to confirm to them that Šimon was dead. He was not capable of describing to them exactly how he died. Šimon's death had been so dreadful he was unable to repeat what the witness had told him. That night Vendulka crept into Karla's bed and they fell asleep curled up together, as they had always done when they were feeling wretched. They would never discover in which of the mass graves Šimon was buried.

In spite of the distress of their loss, life started to get back to normal. Vendulka started attending school again after leaving it against her will in 1940. As she had lost almost all her clothing, she sewed herself some new clothes out of curtains. She loved being able to run herself a hot bath every evening and lie under the water listening to the bubbles of the bath foam bursting. She was also delighted to discover that her closest friends from Terezín – Kitty, Dáša and Líza – had also survived the war. They had all been in Auschwitz and returned to Prague. They helped Vendulka forget the past.

She constantly suffered anxiety attacks, particularly at moments when she was alone. She therefore made an effort always to be in someone's company. She would go to the cinema with her pals or invite them home. Sometimes they would study together, but most of the time they ran around town and made the most of their newly-restored freedom. No longer did they have to wear a yellow star. They could take the tram and have a chat in a restaurant, as well as ride through the streets of Prague on their bikes and play the volleyball they enjoyed so much. They loved dancing and sitting around in cafés, and doing everything that had been denied them in concentration camp – including the first flirtations and dates.

Vendulka first met up with Jan Lukas in the autumn of 1945 after he was discharged from hospital. One of the first photographs he took was of the visit to Prague by General Dwight D. Eisenhower. No announcement was made of the time and place of the visit, but people in the street recognised the general and welcomed him so enthusiastically that the traffic was blocked for a considerable length of time. When Jan Lukas knocked on the door of the apartment on Lodecká Street and Karla opened it, he silently hugged her and Vendulka for a long time. The photo of the family group that he had promised to take after the war was no longer possible. They started to visit each other and Jan introduced his girlfriend Milena to them.

"We're engaged," he declared proudly.

Vendulka immediately fell for Milena. She liked her easy-going manner and cheerful nature that occasionally bordered on playful flippancy. The wedding took place on 26 June 1946 in the Clam-Gallas Palace. It was a secret affair – Lukas's mother did not approve of the marriage, considering Milena, who was an orphan and had no dowry, to be an unsuitable match. So only a small group of their closest friends joined them at the palace. The witnesses were Vladimír Peroutka, the head of the Melantrich publishing house, and Antonín Štembera, the husband of Lukas's sister Eliška – although even she was kept in the dark about the wedding in case she let her mother into the secret. At the last minute they were joined by the actor Vlastimil Brodský, who had bumped into one of the wedding guests on the street and hadn't wanted to miss the chance of congratulating the newlyweds.

It was a a joyful time. They would all go off on outings together, go skating, or visit their favourite resort of Medlov. Lukas's postwar photographs are redolent of new optimism, energy, and joy. This is evident in a photo taken one Sunday afternoon in 1947, which they spent in the company of Vendulka and Karla at a bathing spot by the Berounka river.

By then Milena was already expecting their first child – their daughter Jana. Milena smiles as she turns towards her husband. She is wearing sun glasses with white frames, and her face and low-cut neckline are bathed in the intense summer sunlight. Vendulka stands above her, her head to one side, drying her wavy hair with a towel. She smiles, her eyes half-closed, and the river glitters behind her silhouette. There is something boyish about her expression and stance, but her figure is already turning into that of a beautiful adult woman. And Jan Lukas has clearly noticed.

He began to use her more and more often as a photographic model for popular magazines. In his coloured advertisement for "Milena BRONZ", Vendulka is leaning her chin on her hand and looking to one side dreamily. In another she is floating on her back in a one-piece swimming costume, surrounded by foaming water. "It is love that drives the trout against the beguiling waves. Where can sweet dreams be fulfilled?" was the lyrical description appended to the photo by the magazine's editor. It was almost as if there had never been a war.

Jan Lukas was very conscious of the political changes, however. Although his books of photographs lack any depictions of the expulsion of three million Czech Germans, this was probably because the first expulsions occurred when he was still confined to his hospital bed, and the later ones took place at time when he was planning his marriage and had other things on his mind. In November 1945, however, he photographed an elderly couple standing at a bank counter. They have come to change money during the first post-war monetary reform. Their diminutive figures are almost dwarfed by the bank manager's huge counter and give the impression of powerlessness. Jan Lukas included the photo in his collection *Prague Diary 1938–1965* and appended the comment: "Current bank notes, savings and insurance policies were suddenly worthless."

He once more took to the streets with camera in hand, capturing on his photographs major historical events and how they impacted the lives of ordinary people. Those photos included a portrait of K.H. Frank, one-time bookseller who served as Minister of State for the "Protectorate of Bohemia and Moravia", photographed when he was standing in court listening to the voice of an interpreter over his headphones. He was sentenced to death and executed on 22 May 1946 for war crimes and his active role in the destruction of Lidice and Ležáky. Unlike others convicted in the post-war period, Frank had the great advantage of being defended at his trial by the best Czech defence counsel, Kamill Resler – even though it was to no avail. The other defendants in the retribution trials were less fortunate. The so-called "major" retribution decree adopted by the Czech government-in-exile while still in London stipulated that there was no appeal possible against the verdicts of the extraordinary people's courts set up chiefly to try cases of high treason. What was unusual in Czechoslovakia compared to other European countries was the combination of refusal of appeal and the stipulation that executions be carried out within two hours of the verdict. That period could be extended to three hours if the convicted person so requested. Presidential clemency was therefore almost impossible to request, and less than five percent of those who requested it were successful. The number of executions in the Czech lands was consequently the highest of any country in Europe – 723 people were sentenced to death and 686 of them were executed (in France only 791 of the seven thousand sentenced to death were actually executed).

The so-called "minor" retribution decree, which was intended to deal with minor offences – such as "offending national feelings", improper conduct or public indecency – with which Czechs were mostly charged, led to the investigation of a further 180,000 people, of whom over a quarter were punished. That figure does not include the "cleansing commissions" in theatres, factories, ministries, local municipal bodies and elsewhere. These affected tens of thousands more people, whose indictment meant they were denied a certificate of national reliability and consequently lost their jobs or their right to vote.

But neither the major nor the minor retribution decrees provided for penalties against wrongful denunciation. Anybody could denounce someone and there was no risk of their being prosecuted if they lied. Some judges, journalists and politicians, including Pavel Tigrid and Ladislav Feierabend, criticised that legal concept and pointed to the abuse of the retribution laws by people pursuing personal vengeance, but such voices were in the minority.

The Czech government expected that the overwhelming majority of those condemned to death would be Germans and did not allow for the possibility that the Czechs' desire for retribution, justice and revenge would be directed just as strongly against their own people. It was unwilling to rescind its decisions, however, mostly out of fear that the Communists would make use of the retribution laws against their political opponents, although that did indeed happen, but several years later.

In March 1948, the Communists revived the retribution courts and deprived tens of thousands of people of their right to vote, and in subsequent years the retribution laws were the basis of show trials used to get rid of their critics and opponents. In those days the paths of Vendulka and Jan Lukas once more diverged for many years.

Home at last. (Vendulka in a snow fight with Milena, no date, photo Jan Lukas)

(95)

As if there had never been a war. (1947, photo Jan Lukas)

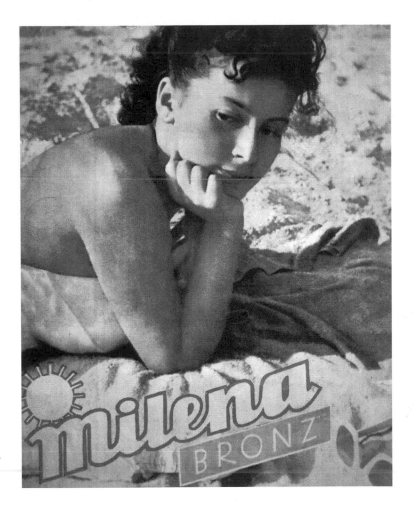

Modelling for Lukas's magazine and fashion photos (1947, photo Jan Lukas)

(97)

Lively debate. (The comedians Suchý and Šlitr at the Lukases' flat,
1962, archive of Helena Lukas)

So we still have enough time. (Milena and Jan Lukas before they left Czechoslovakia, 1962, archive of Helena Lukas)

Flight to Freedom

"It was easy to recognise a Communist: he scowls when others are rejoicing," Jan Lukas wrote about one of the photos he took at the Sokol gymnastics festival that took place from 19 to 27 July 1948. It was several months after the Communist takeover of power, and the gymnastics rally in Prague turned into a mass protest against the emerging dictatorship. It was the last free protest for many years.

On Lukas's photograph thousands of people in the streets wave small Czech and American flags and carry portraits of Masaryk and Beneš, despite the fact that the latter had abdicated a few weeks before and by then Klement Gottwald was head of state. Gottwald was obliged to suffer in silence the refusal of Sokol members to obey the command "Eyes left!" and they walked past the viewing stand looking the other way.

People in the streets chanted anti-Communist slogans and members of State Security and the People's Militia ran among them angrily tearing the American flags out of their hands. Almost two hundred Sokol members were arrested and taken off for interrogation.

"Those who rely on the regime have something in common", was Jan Lukas's comment on another of his photos. It depicted a number of Communists with the label "steward" on their lapels. Whereas the people around them were enjoying themselves and cheerfully waving their arms over their heads the Communists are standing with pursed lips and folded arms. The Communists soon exacted their revenge. The Action Committees of the National Front expelled almost 11,000 members from Sokol branches and then merged the Sokol with the unitary socialist P.E. organisation, thereby silencing it for 41 long years, along with other independent organisations and associations, as well as the political opposition and critics. When, two months later, Jan Lukas photographed Edvard Beneš's funeral, which was accompanied by thousands of people with tears in their eyes, the "stewards" were standing in the streets with rifles in their hands.

Vendulka and Karla saw how the regime was treating its opponents and were reluctant to lose their new-found freedom once more.

"We must leave while we still can," Karla announced one day to her daughter during their evening meal. At first Vendulka didn't want to leave. She had made new friends since returning from concentration camp and didn't want to lose them again. However, the fear of the malice and violence that she observed on the streets of Prague convinced her.

In reply to their application for emigration passports they received a letter stating: "The Ministry has studied the matter in the light of protection of the domestic labour market and also from the social point of view and has no objection to its being issued."

They decided in favour of Canada. After the war some of their relatives and friends who had managed to survive had gone there, including Věra, one of the childhood friends that Vendulka and Karla had met on the death march. Her sister Hana had also survived the march but died a few days later from typhus.

Karla and Vendulka first had to undergo a medical examination and submit a certificate of their moral integrity, as well prove to the Czechoslovak state that they owed nothing in tax and owned no movable property previously owned by Germans, Hungarians or collaborators. The emigration passports issued by the National Security Directorate were received by them on 3 May 1948, and they were valid for two years. They allowed them to travel via Germany, France, Belgium, Holland and England. In the end Vendulka's concern about her departure was eased when she learned that all her friends from Terezín had also decided to emigrate – Kitty headed to Australia, while Dáša and Líza left for the USA. There was nothing in Prague to retain her any more apart from Jan Lukas and his wife Milena. They said farewell once more at the apartment on Lodecká Street and promised to see each other again soon. It would take almost twenty years.

On their way to Canada they stopped off at some relatives in London, who tried to persuade them to stay, but Vendulka and Karla wanted to go as far as possible from the old continent, away from the horrors whose echoes and shadows haunted them at every turn. Europe was recovering only very slowly from the war, and as they travelled they could see how its cities still bore the scars of air raids and fires.

They crossed the ocean by plane, and a few weeks later a ship arrived with part of their Prague home – cupboards and personal effects. They were bound for Montreal, where there was a large community of Czech immigrants. The early days were difficult, but after what they had been through they quite enjoyed the various complications. Karla found a job as a housekeeper in the home of some fairly wealthy Canadians and Vendulka started to attend art school. She was therefore able to follow up on what she had studied under Friedl Dicker-Brandeis at Terezín.

She did everything she could to conceal the fact she was Jewish and had endured concentration camp. While she was still in Prague she had been received into the Roman Catholic church and chose a Christian name in addition to her given name. In America she had the number tattooed on her forearm surgically removed, and resolved never to speak about her experience. Initially this was also out of fear that things could change for the worse again. She was afraid that if she was arrested again and imprisoned somewhere that she would not survive this time. She therefore tried not to step out of line or draw attention to herself. She wanted to be accepted somewhere unreservedly at last, just as she was.

She soon achieved this – at least partly. She met a charismatic Czech doctor, Alexander Hořava. He was tall and good-looking. She was impressed by the fact that he had managed to achieve success in a competitive environment and was now a highly regarded physician. She fell in love with him at first sight. They were married in 1953, and five years later they moved to Columbus, Ohio, where Alexander had obtained a grant from the hospital there. Karla went with them too, of course; Vendulka could not imagine their living apart. Their homes were just a few minutes away from each other by car and scarcely a day passed when they did not see each other, or had a telephone conversation at least.

During the first years after their arrival in Columbus, Vendulka made a living from drawing advertisements for fashion houses. They were mostly black-and-white drawings against a coloured background – figures of elegant women in beautiful costumes with handbags over their shoulders. After a few years, however, she had to give up this work as she was fully occupied with the care of two daughters. Susan was born in 1957 and Kathy three years later.

Karla accompanied her on walks with the pram, and she helped mind the children when Vendulka needed a rest. They almost never spoke together about the past. From time to time Karla would recall some detail, but Vendulka only wanted to look towards the future. The same was true of Kitty, Dáša and Líza, whom she would occasionally meet in Las Vegas or Florida. They would always chat long into the night, all the time laughing about something. They mostly spoke about their children and their present joys. They longed to go on being cheerful and leave the wartime events buried deep in their subconscious.

A Time of Mammoth Plans

The society magazines that Jan Lukas had contributed to for many years were abolished. They had propagated a decadent, bourgeois lifestyle that was incompatible with the needs and aims of the working proletariat. Lukas's photographs suddenly teemed with five-pointed stars, posters of political bosses, Uncle Joe Stalin with his moustache, women milking cows or driving tractors. Communist iconography was inescapable. It adorned the façades of hotels, tramcars, streets and cowsheds. Lukas commented on it ironically as was his wont. He had no other option anyway.

"It was the start of a time of mammoth plans. (...) But the posters with the new leaders were the only things of gigantic dimensions," he commented on one of the photos.

Fortunately he was able to go freelance and make extra money by photographing weddings and taking family portraits. In order to publish abroad he had sign up with the state-run agency Artia, like other artists. The fees paid in foreign currency then went mostly into the coffers of the Communist regime.

Jan Lukas did not openly oppose the regime, but Communist ideology was anathema to him. He had already started to think about emigrating in February 1948, but he still believed that the political situation might improve. In addition, his second daughter Helena was born in 1950, so he put off the idea of emigration.

Milena was more determined. She felt herself stifled under the Communist regime and she pleaded with her husband that they should leave as soon as possible. After one such argument she reproached him that she would never get to see any foreign countries. Lukas then walked out of the apartment and returned with a voucher for an excursion to Greece organised by the state travel agency Čedok. The day prior to their departure, however, they received notification that they had been excluded from the excursion as there was no more room on the ship. Lukas inquired whether they would let them go if he arranged for a cabin himself. The Čedok staff replied in amusement that they couldn't prevent him doing so, of course. So, through friends in Greece, Jan did indeed find a vacant cabin, and he and Milena set off on their journey after all, and they enjoyed more luxurious conditions that the other travellers from Prague. They had to leave their daughters in Prague, however, as hostages.

In 1953 there was a glimmer of hope that the regime might fall. That year the Soviet leader Stalin and Czechoslovak President Gottwald died one after the other – on 5 and 14 March. "God forgive me, but that was a joyous week," Jan Lukas commented in his *Prague Diary*. During Christmas that year he photographed his younger daughter as the Statue of Liberty holding up a sparkler in place of the torch, while her older sister Jana is perusing a photographic book about New York with a photograph of the original statue. He sent a copy of the photo to his friends as a Christmas greeting. But the sparkler in Helena's hand extinguished itself as quickly as the prospects for a happier future.

Compared to the rest of the population Jan Lukas had more room to manoeuvre and scope to obtain for himself, by sheer obstinacy, a certain degree of freedom, at least. Inspiring and free-thinking intellectuals and artists would meet up in his apartment in Mělnická Street and debate politics late into the night over wine and cigarettes, and bet on how long the regime would still survive. On one of Lukas's photos, he is surrounded by the poet Emanuel Frynta, the writer Ladislav Fikar, the painter Kamil Lhoták, and the jazz composer Jan Rychlík. On another, Lukas is with the actor and theatre company director Jiří Suchý. They had become friends at the Reduta jazz club where they both used to go for a drink, and the young actor used to sing. Lukas showed him a couple of shots he had taken of the actor's performances unbeknownst to him, and Suchý was intrigued. Eventually Suchý took him to the Semafor Theatre and Lukas spent many afternoons there with his daughters Jana and Helena, photographing the rehearsals and performances. Helena even accompanied Jiří Suchý, and in one performance she danced the Charleston with him.

So Jan Lukas could not complain about lack of interest in his work. At the Expo 58 world fair in Brussels, the Laterna Magika black-light theatre projected his photos and the international jury awarded them a gold medal. Four years later, the State Publishing House of Literature, Music and Arts published a monography bearing his name – Jan Lukas – which featured sixty reproductions of his photos from the years 1931–1961. The book was also issued in an English-French-German edition.

But the way the Communist regime treated someone with Lukas's talent is illustrated by the curious fate of his photographic book *Moscow*. The Artia publishing house was initially planning to bring out the collection of 128 documentary photographs from the turn of the 1960s in a German-language edition, but the Soviet embassy found the image of the Communist metropolis as seen by Lukas's lens too sombre. The terrified publishing house therefore pulped all 10,000 copies of the already printed book. A year later, a British publishing house ordered the same book, so 20,000 copies were printed in an English-language edition.

In spite of his successes, Jan Lukas did not stop thinking about emigrating. He finally decided to leave after managing to make a trip to the USA in 1964. On that occasion, he headed for New York with his younger daughter Helena. As before, he had to leave his wife and other daughter at home.

New York held him spellbound. He spent four weeks dashing around its streets. He photographed chess players in the park, orthodox Jews with kippahs and sidelocks, half-naked hippies, the pretty boys in Little Italy, black hipsters with cigarettes in their mouths, a beautiful girl with a pug dog in Washington Square. A colourful world, in total contrast to socialist realism and its mindless iconography under the Communist regime. He visited many of his friends there, particularly the photographer and film director Alexander Hackenschmied, who had left for the USA before war broke out and had changed his surname to Hammid. He also proposed to Karla and Vendulka that they should meet up, but Vendulka was busy looking after her children and wasn't in a position to make a trip at short notice.

While Jan Lukas was imbibing the atmosphere of the city and sating himself with scenes that he found exotic, his daughter Helena was walking around Manhattan with Hackenschmied's mother, eating ice-creams and drinking gallons of milk, so that she put on 14 kilos. When they returned a month later, Milena and Jana didn't recognise her.

"Let's leave," Lukas declared to his wife as they were falling asleep the night of his return. "There's no point in waiting."

The Only Option

A turquoise Volga car approached the Yugoslav-Italian border. It was August 1965. The sun beat down, and customs officers in their white caps leaned wearily on the frontier barrier. Jan Lukas had spent several days driving round the border crossings in the area and observing from a distance how each of them was guarded. Finally he chose the border near the Slovenian town of Šempeter pri Gorici. The distance separating the two frontiers is the shortest here and one of the frontier barriers did not close properly, so that it was twenty or so centimetres higher than the other. If they'd have to break through there was less danger of his wife and daughter being injured. In addition, they had been joined in the car by a family friend Lucie Chytilová and her daughters Anna and Helena, who were eight and six years old.

The Volga joined the queue of cars and slowly moved towards the armed customs officers. Jan asked Milena not to speak to him as he needed to concentrate on choosing the right moment. Just as they arrived level with the customs officer, the man turned his back on their car for a few moment. "I'd go for it," Milena whispered. Jan pressed the accelerator pedal to the floor, gripped the steering wheel firmly, and leaned back in his seat. "Heads down, girls!" he warned his passengers.

The turquoise Volga broke through the barrier and sped across no-man's-land towards the Italian customs post. The little girls in the back seats ducked and only Jana disobediently looked through the rear windscreen to see if the Yugoslavs were following them. But instead of the anticipated gunshots, there were just the shouts of astonished soldiers. From the other side, their Italian colleagues were waving to them and gesturing at them not to take any action. The people in the Volga were "theirs" now.

Milena and Lucie burst into tears of happiness, or simply because they were no longer afraid.

"Didn't we escape, Mummy?" Anna asked when she saw the tears on her mother's face. At that moment they all burst out laughing...

After the preliminary asylum procedures, the Lukas's ended up in the San Sabba refugee camp in Trieste, which had served as a concentration camp during World War II. They spent three weeks there, during which Jana celebrated her eighteenth birthday. Then they were transferred to a refugee camp at Capua, where they spent another eight months. Their accommodation was one room in a metal portable cabin, furnished with four beds, a cupboard and a stove. They stuffed the mattresses with straw to get rid of the bed bugs. The food was meagre: pasta twice a week. They supplemented it by buying cheese, fruit and honey, and occasionally they went into town for a pizza or a grilled chicken. There was also a flea market every week, where lots of used clothes were on sale, so Jana and Helena had fun choosing clothes and altering them, as well as running after boys and learning Italian.

After so many years of the oppressive Communist regime, they felt as if they were in heaven. They visited ancient Pompeii, Sorrento, Amalfi, Naples and the Isle of Capri. Lukas documented the family's new life: conditions in the camp, and the hustle and bustle of the street. At the Vatican he took a portrait of Josef Beran, the exiled Archbishop of Prague, who was shortly afterwards appointed cardinal by the pope. Permission to take the portrait was obtained by Lukas' acquaintance, the exiled People's Party politician Bohumír Bunža, who had to flee Czechoslovakia straight after the Communist coup in February 1948 and did not see his family for twenty years. He was sentenced to death in his absence by the regime.

Vendulka learnt about the Lukases' emigration at the end of March 1966. She managed to discover their address and sent them a letter. By that time the family had once more changed their place of residence and moved to New York, this time for good.

Dear Honza,
Pleasant surprises await us at different times in our lives. And to-
day, which brought news of you and your family, is one of them.
After many years, my Mom started to correspond with Janka
Součková (actually she has a different surname now, and maybe
you don't even remember her) and in her last letter she asked
about you. The reply came this morning saying we're nearer to
you than she is, as you're in New York. We were so delighted that
we dashed to the telephone and called an acquaintance in N.Y.
who knows the whole Czech colony. A short while later she called
to say that unfortunately you're not there yet but might be there
very soon, and I sincerely hope you will be. It's awful that you
poor folk are stuck in some camp somewhere, but the main thing
is that you're almost there. When we arrived in Canada I was
convinced that it was part of a good upbringing to spend time
in a camp, but that was such a long time ago. I was ashamed of
being one of the few people who were spared it. Honza, please,
please write to me if you need some money. God forbid that I
should cause you offence. I've no idea what situation you are in,
but if I can help you, please write to me straight away.
Maybe you won't recall, but Jiřina told me that you received
a letter from the camp in Germany and you immediately took off
the sweater you were wearing and rummaged around for all sorts
of things and sent us them in a parcel. I will never forget and will
be grateful to you for as long as I live. I only mention it because
I want you to realise that it would give me enormous pleasure to
help you. I am not enclosing anything in this letter as I'm not
sure it will reach you, but please don't make a big thing of it and
write, OK?
I can't wait for us to have a chat on the phone. I'd love to
see all of you, but I don't often get to N.Y., unfortunately. I have
three little offspring that I can't really foist onto Mom and simply
skedaddle, but I hope you'll come and visit us. Mom sends her
love and greetings to you all and is hoping to see you. She hasn't
aged much and really looks great. She's full of energy and I re-
ally don't know what I'd do without her. She lives in a tiny little
house with a cat about ten minutes away, and cheerfully spoils
her grandchildren as much as possible. We, on the other hand,
have a house as big as Karlštejn castle, which I myself chose, un-
fortunately, so I have no one else to blame. I see I'm starting to

write all sorts of nonsense. There are a thousand things I'd like to ask you, but let them wait for when you'll be here. Dearest Jan, write me a few lines to say how you are. A thousand wishes to Milena and the girls, I look forward to seeing you very, very soon (I'm not sure whether I can still write correctly in Czech).

Yours,
Vendula

PS: I've just realised that I saw your elder little girl when she was about a week old and she was the most beautiful baby I'd ever seen – or at least until my Susan was born!

Meanwhile State Security (StB) in Czechoslovakia was up in arms. By mid-October 1965 it had opened a file on Jan Lukas with the code name "SAKUL" and initiated proceedings against him and Milena, as well as their daughter Jana, who had just come of age, for the criminal offence of "unauthorised desertion of the republic".

"Lukas had been preparing for desertion of the republic for a long time and was only waiting for an opportunity when he would be permitted to travel abroad with his whole family," it states in the file of the investigation headed by master warrant officer Josef Lejnar of State Security. "He only feigned a positive attitude to our state and social system. The motive for his actions is clearly the thought of more advantageous conditions for so-called free enterprise, and his entire family conformed to his views and decisions. The social danger of his actions is aggravated by the fact that he prepared them in advance, carried them out with premeditation, and apparently influenced his whole family not to return to the Czechoslovak Socialist Republic, and that fact can be misused to intensify hostile propaganda against the republic."

The only person the StB could take revenge on was Lukas's mother Alžběta, who was then 77 years old. She was forced to leave the apartment in Mělnická Street, and the secret police did not even allow her to take with her photographs of her family and friends. She moved to her daughter's in Pardubice and tried to claim back at least some of her personal property.

"Would you kindly inform me where the furnishings of my room and others things are to be found and what I am to do now. These things might seem old-fashioned to you, but they are the surroundings in which I lived and there are memories attached to every item," she wrote to the department of the State Security in charge. *"We old people might be odd, but we have an emotional attachment to things connected with our memories and I can't believe it is possible that everything I had could be confiscated. I am already of an advanced age and have not been well in the recent period, so I am unable to travel to Prague to find out whether my room and its furnishings have remained where they were as promised, and where the other things are. I find it hard to imagine that I should be penalised for something for which I am not responsible."*

She received the following terse reply from a representative of the Ministry of the Interior.

"When you state in your letter that you received a promise that you will be informed about the disposal of the property, this has no basis in fact."

So the family album kept by Lukas's parents and grandparents was pulped, and nothing is known of the fate of rare pictures by Kamil Lhoták, Alois Fišárek, Josef Čapek and František Tichý. Lost also were Jan Lukas's two hundred thousand negatives, which he could not take with him, as he had nowhere to hide them during his escape. He hid only the most valuable ones at the home of some friends, who later brought them to America – including the negatives of the photos of Vendulka and her parents.

Lukas explained it himself as follows in an interview with him: "I put in my pocket what I considered important... it was a bit like going for a swim. You hold onto things – books and magazines... I almost said to myself that perhaps I left in order to get rid of it all."

Jan Lukas and his family flew to America from Rome on 16 June 1966 on an Alitalia flight full of refugees. It was a direct flight to New York's John F. Kennedy airport. Shortly before, they had all received their Green Cards permitting them residence in the New World. They were welcomed at the airport by Hammid's wife Hela and his mother, together with the journalist Ivo Ducháček and his wife Helena. They all stood holding a sign saying: "The Lukases are in New York." Jan Lukas subsequently described his departure from Czechoslovakia in an article in the exile journal *Svědectví* entitled *Why I chose exile*. The text was published in 1966:

That was one of the first questions Italian immigration officials asked me in Trieste after our escape from Yugoslavia. I answered them more or less as follows: "Sorry, but I was not able to before. It was not possible, at least not with the entire family. And yet during the past eighteen years I've almost thought of nothing else but getting out of the country. Now I've finally achieved it. So we're here, and we want to go to America."

In Prague I would tell my friends ad nauseam that I wanted to leave, that I wanted to live and not vegetate. The joke is that somehow no one took it seriously. The same applied to my opinions. I was thought to be "progressive" (a tiresome concept, since even paralysis can be progressive, as we all know), so whenever I said that the only option open to me was to escape, my friends would joke: "If you didn't know him better, you'd think he meant it!"

Moreover, various circumstances and my personal situation only fuelled their scepticism. Above all, the fact that I was well-off in Prague. I had a better standard of living than the great majority of people in Czechoslovakia. By and large I earned five times more that the statistical national average, which doesn't mean, of course – and that is one of the absurdities of life in Czechoslovakia –that my wife didn't have to search for something decent for Sunday lunch. Another instance: I had a really nice Volga for which I had paid several times the average wage of an average worker, but when I went for a drive somewhere in that car, in luxurious comfort, I generally couldn't afford a lunch of the same standard.

But I'll begin at the beginning, or almost at the beginning. From 1948 to 1953 I lived as a freelance. In those days the old currency was still valid and there were still people who had money, so one could at least survive financially, as some former wealthy people would pay for me to photograph their children, weddings, or Christmas celebrations. That was important; I didn't have to go and work in an office, attend meetings, spout crap, or collaborate. In short, I managed to cope as they say.

But then in March 1953, the "week of death" arrived and they buried Stalin and Gottwald in quick succession, and monetary reform was not long in coming – namely in June. People lost their savings, nobody had anything, and certainly not for photographs of family occasions. I had to "come to terms financially with the given circumstances" as they say. (Escape was out of the question: I had two small children and foreign travel was banned.) An opportunity arose to work in the state film industry, on the fringe, as it were, for the magazine Kino. Moreover, after the death of Stalin, the total isolation in which we lived in those days started – slowly, but surely– to fracture. And there was the beginning of a shift of some kind – in my branch, at least.

Czechoslovakia started to send stuff to western trade fairs, so "bourgeois photography" became respectable, and smiling women driving tractors and exemplary cow milkers were no longer the only subjects, and there were now slightly more real people and things, such as pretty young women, for instance. In Prague they remembered the people who used to know how to photograph them, so I was able to make use of my older work as well as my new stuff. Eventually I was even able to terminate my employment contract with the state film organisation and work freelance once more as a member of the Artists' Union.

(…) They will be searching for the motives and reasons why I went into exile. I can be sure of that because when I was in Prague, whenever anyone from our circle managed to escape they would always talk about it and say: OK, but what was his real reason for it? And they would look for every possible and impossible reason to rationalise why we hadn't escaped, why we hadn't taken the decision, and always were slightly ashamed that we hadn't taken the decision. And people would strenuously seek some blemish in the character of the person who escaped, something that would belittle his decision and action.

Why did I choose exile? There were enough motives and reasons to fill a novel. I left because from the outset I didn't want to live in a country where the rules of the game were unknown, where "you're honoured as a saint one day, and the next day you're a blackguard," where uncertainty about how things will

(114)

be in the evening, let alone next year, turns a citizen into a puppet. I didn't want my children to live in this country of arbitrary rule. I also left because I wanted to test and assess myself, but not in the sense of political screening.

For my work I needed some kind of objective measure of what I was capable of, how much I could do, some kind of clearcut criterion. And such an authentic and often harsh criterion can be found only in an open society, in a society which at least to some extent – but in all aspects of life – is rational, protects the rules of the game, and maintains normality. So far everything in our country tends to be abnormal.

Up to now in the field of art and artists the situation was as follows: the writer would write something, the artist would paint something, and the film maker would make a film, and the Party, the comrades and the party press would shoot it down and slander it, and possibly the censor would ban it – ensuring its success regardless of its quality, because the creator became a persecuted individual. Alternatively, the Party, the comrades and the party press would approve the work and even praise it. And you'd say to yourself: You see, I'm so good that even the comrades "at the top" had to acknowledge it. In short, everything is fine, whether the artist is slandered or praised. Abnormal, isn't it? The artist makes good money, and is therefore excellent; or he slogs away in poverty – and that's also proof that he is excellent.

Every other one of us is "world class" – or was until quite recently. Under Stalinism, circles and groups were formed, drinking partners who used to get together in the evening and slap each other on the back, saying: "If we had a chance to show the world what we're capable of they'd all sit up." I don't want to downplay the situation of artists in our country. On the contrary, I simply want to say that there is a yearning in our country in the field of literature and art for confrontation with the literature and art of the western world, while at the same time there is a kind of fear of that confrontation. Because confrontation in all areas of human endeavour means a normalisation of relationships and a more stringent classification of values.

Moreover, the situation in our country is complicated by the fact that people who until recently only knew socialist realism (and of the crudest kind) in art suddenly retrained as avantgarde artists. Now nothing is lopsided enough for them, as one Prague painter put it. All the more so, since they have convinced themselves that the party has convinced itself that in the final analysis not much will happen in the state or even in art if artists paint the way they see fit. Let them do what they like, lopsided or not, so long as it doesn't say anything too obvious about the truth.

The truth! Of course people know what it is, broadly speaking, but they cope with it at various levels, so to speak, as necessary, according to their degree of courage or cowardice, according to the situation, and with regard to others... In Prague nowadays it means in practice that people are extremely careful with their truth, and from time to time, at moments of increased danger, they stuff it deep into their suitcase among the dirty clothes, like contraband at a customs post. It is necessary – or so they say – to be two-faced. But a member of the intelligentsia is (is supposed to be?) intelligent, and so knows all too well what he should be ashamed of – such as grumbling about the regime and cursing it, and then going hunting on the weekend with the top bosses of the same regime.

How can one make sense of it and cope with it? I always wanted to escape it because I could see no other way out, and because I fear that a return to normal life and normal human relations is going to take so long. And what confirmed my decision to leave was a realisation, probably only at the subconscious level, that among those who were and are my friends it is always absolutely clear who stands where, that our shared barricade is divided by hundreds of lesser boundaries accumulated by indifference to various values, or the extent of courage or cowardice.

It was easy to recognise a Communist: he scowls when others are rejoicing. (Prague, 1948, photo Jan Lukas)

One day it will come true. (New Year's card of Helena and Jan Lukas, 1954, photo Jan Lukas)

In the refugee camp, but free. (The Lukases at Capua in Italy, 1966, archive of Helena Lukas)

The first trip to America... (Fish market, New York, 1964,
photo Jan Lukas)

...was a foretoken of exile and a new home. (From the Brooklyn Promenade, New York,1974, photo Jan Lukas)

Always something to discover. (Jan Lukas in his Manhattan apartment, 1995, photo Josef Moucha)

Real Life

Temperatures during the summer holidays of 1966 broke records. The streets of New York shimmered in the heat and everyone tried to find some welcome shade. The Lukases spent the first two weeks in Alexander Hammid's apartment as they tried to get their bearings in the new country. Lots of other Czech acquaintances lived between 87th and 89th streets, so it felt a bit like home. They rented a small apartment on West 86th Street, just a short distance from Central Park. Jan Lukas wrote to his closest friends, including Vendulka, to say that things were fine. As soon as she'd opened and read the letter Vendulka called him on the telephone. Seventeen years had passed since he last heard her voice.

"How did you get out? Who are you living with?" the questions came pouring out of her. He described how he was trying to find work but that it wasn't easy as he didn't know his way around New York yet and everything was new to him.

"Listen, Honza, send Helena to us," she said, interrupting him. "She can spend the summer vacation with us. She'll learn more English and it'll make things easier for you."

Lukas eagerly accepted, and a few days later his younger daughter was sitting in a plane at New York's La Guardia airport heading for Columbus.

Vendulka's life had undergone several changes in recent years. Her first marriage to Alexander Hořava did not last due to mutual differences, and in 1962 they divorced. Moreover, her husband suffered from serious health problems and died prematurely at the age of thirty-nine. A year after his death Vendulka got married for the second time. Her new husband was also a doctor, Alexander's hospital colleague Jacob Wise Old. They bought a house in the opulent neighbourhood of Upper Arlington in Columbus, with a large garden and swimming pool. In 1965 their son Leigh was born, and eight years later, their daughter Christina.

When Helena flew in for her summer holiday, she felt as if she was in a castle. She was given her own guest room with a large bed. She quickly changed into her swimming costume and went with Vendulka's daughters Susan and Kathy for a swim. They were eight and six years old and were good swimmers, and Helena admired how fearlessly they dived into the pool from the diving board. They gave little Leigh the nickname Lolly. He was not yet one year old and they carried him in their arms and played with him on a blanket in the garden.

Vendulka fell for Helena. She could see Jan's features in her face and the moments they spent together revived her memories of his visits to them in Karlovy Vary and at the apartment in Lodecká Street. She took Helena downtown to buy material and together they came up with a design for a new skirt and dress, which she helped Helena to sew. On one outing Vendulka took her to German Village, where she usually brought bread, whose taste was similar to Czech bread and reminded her of home. Even so she told her daughters not to buy German products and never to buy a German car.

In the end Helena returned to New York a week early. She had heard that the Beatles were due to perform there, and she very much wanted to hear them live. Her journey turned out to be an adventure, however. She flew via Chicago, where she had a two-hour stopover. She wanted to take advantage of the time, so she took a bus downtown to see the sights. But her excursion went over time and she missed her flight. Jan Lukas frantically called Vendulka and together they tried to discover where Helena had got lost. She arrived by the next flight a few hours later.

She and her father attended the Beatles concert together. Over fifty thousand fans were crammed into Shea Stadium, which was usually used for baseball games. The ticket cost five dollars, which was quite a lot of money at that time, and the organisers grossed the highest takings in history. While his daughter joined in with the Fab Four singing *Twist and Shout, A Hard Day's Night, Help* and *I Feel Fine*, her father spent almost the entire concert with his back to the stage photographing the enraptured faces of the audience.

Jan was then fifty years old. He found himself in a new country and had to begin at the beginning once more. "Trying to establish yourself here in photography is like spitting in the ocean," he sighed, in an interview with the Czech language magazine *Západ*. His previous successes counted for nothing. In that far more competitive environment he had to prove afresh his outstanding talent. He did the rounds of magazine editors and publishers and some of them published his photos, but not in the sort of settings he wanted. He earned money by photographing weddings and taking portraits as he had in Czechoslovakia. The family budget was in the hands of Milena, who, after a few smaller jobs, found employment as an accountant in a bank.

By now their elder daughter Jana also helped them. She got a job with the Harry Winston jewellery firm on Fifth Avenue, where she sorted diamonds. This was a prestigious company, where Aristotle Onassis would buy an engagement ring for Jacqueline Kennedy.

"Why should I worry, when I've got three women with me!" Jan would declare with a smile.

He believed he would eventually gain a toehold. He used to say of himself that he was already an American back home and didn't view emigration as any fundamental change. His life simply consisted of separate periods. He divided them into three main chapters. The first was the period of the Liberated Theatre of Voskovec and Werich, where he spent all his free time before the war. The second was the period of the Semafor Theatre, which he was involved in from its beginnings, and where he often took his daughters behind the scenes. And now the American period had arrived, and once more he took it in his stride. It never occurred to him to regret anything. He walked around New York taking photos for himself, and soon he knew the city like the back of his hand. At the beginning he had the help of Czech friends who escaped to the USA before the war: the journalist Ferdinand Peroutka, Jiří Voskovec and the aforementioned Alexander Hammid, with whom in 1967 he worked on the film US, a pictorial essay about the United States of America. A year later he himself acted as a guide to the "city that never sleeps" for a young visitor from Prague – who had a small moustache and a lit cigarette always between his fingers, and had trouble pronouncing his "r"s. His name was Václav Havel, and twenty-one years later he would become President of Czechoslovakia. On Jan Lukas's photographs Havel looks like a Hollywood actor. His eyes are hidden behind sunglasses, and he wears an elegant suit with a fine check, and a white handkerchief in the top pocket. In one photograph he is walking round the lake in Central Park, and on another Lukas captured him in thoughtful conversation with Ferdinand Peroutka, who is sitting in a rocking chair. There is also a photograph of him with Jiří Voskovec, in which Havel is dressed like a hippie with beads round his neck and wearing a jeans jacket. For his journey back to Europe Jan Lukas gave Václav Havel a number of books in English and mailed him another one that he was unable to carry. He then wrote to him on 10 July 1968:

Dear Mr Havel,
I hope you're back from your wanderings and that you safely received two parcels with clothes and books. The girls and ourselves sent them about a month ago, but sometimes it takes a little longer depending on which ship they send it by.
I am also sending a few photographs, because I'm beginning to believe that you meant it seriously with those articles you promised to send me! You personally never meant it anything but seriously, but I wasn't so sure. I'm sure you'll be able to tell who is who on the photographs.
For selfish personal reasons I ought to wish for an end to press freedom here, because I spend such a lot of time reading it all. And nobody pays me for it, as my wife says. That doesn't mean you shouldn't send me, in spite of that, any sort of printed matter you consider worthy of my valuable time.
I look forward to your next visit. Until then I'll have to sort things out here in America a lot, but for the time being I'm personally in the same situation as you. We don't have the right to vote yet.
Best wishes and au revoir

Yours,
Jan Lukas

All the girls send best wishes to you and your wife

Havel's reply arrived shortly before the occupation of Czechoslovakia in August 1968.

Dear Mr Lukas,

Thank you for your kind letter, which finally provoked me to write and tell you what I have long been planning, ever since I got back from America, in fact. You see I was intending to thank you for all the care you lavished on me, and now I have also to thank your daughters for your having arranged for my things to be sent. I felt bad about having made use of you in this way, but I'm sure you recall how hectic my last days in New York were – it was very handy for me that you did it for me and eased my situation at the end of my visit.

(...)

The situation in Czechoslovakia is interesting now. The nation is proudly holding its head up, proud that we will not give in that easily, although at the same time everyone is haunted by the silent fear that Dubček might not keep his nerve and cook up some compromise with the Russians. Nevertheless so far it looks as if he won't – it looks as if they can't shift from the path they've taken without risking a revolution (...) Among other things, a remarkable sign has appeared on Wenceslas Square: RUSSIANS GO HOME.

Please give my best wishes to your wife and daughters.

All the best!

Yours
Václav Havel 24. 7. 1968
Hrádeček

Although Václav Havel was otherwise realistic and prescient in his judgements, on that occasion he got it terribly wrong. The Soviet troops occupied Czechoslovakia for the next twenty years and the Communist Party set about so-called "normalisation" of the situation. This affected Havel too: when he wanted to take a further trip to the USA in 1969 the secret police confiscated his passport a few days before his departure.

Meanwhile Jan Lukas had been contacted by the photographer and curator Cornell Capa, who was a member of Magnum Photos agency, which represented the best photographers from around the world. He recalled that Jan had shown him his photographs after he arrived in the USA, and he offered to organise an exhibition of Lukas's work. It was entitled *Eyewitness Czechoslovakia* and it was supplemented with photos of the Prague Spring by Sonja Bullaty and Angelo Lomeo, and shots of the Soviet invasion supplied by the German reporter Hilmar Pabel. Thanks to the interest in Czechoslovakia at the time, the exhibition was very well received. But interest in events in central Europe, where all protests against the occupation were suddenly silenced, soon waned again and Jan Lukas assigned his photographic diary to his personal archive once more.

In the years that followed he made a living chiefly from photographs for the conservative magazine *National Review*, for which he created over one hundred covers. He became friends with its editor-in-chief, the public intellectual William F. Buckley Jr. Buckley liked Lukas's work so much that he asked him to document his weekly TV show *Firing Line*, which ran without a break from 1966 to 1999. Its guests included members of the country's cultural and artistic elite, ranging from Allan Ginsberg and Ronald Reagan to Noam Chomsky and Margaret Thatcher. Lukas was always there with his camera at the ready.

In his free time he continued to wander New York. On his walks he would bump into André Kertész, a Hungarian photographer he had admired when a beginner. He was inspired by his boundless interest and energy although he was already almost eighty. "He's twenty years older and he still manages to take photographs, so I still have plenty of time," Lukas used to say. Lukas devised new artistic forms and ways of giving his photos an extra dimension and level of meaning. So he would be on the look-out on the New York streets for scenes such as he had photographed years before in Pompeii, or would select quotes from Kafka's unfinished novel *America* and append to them photographic images suggested by the Prague writer's texts, and published them in 1993 with the title *America According to Kafka*. He gave up photography at the end of the 1980s due to ill health.

"When I saw some time in 1989 a young guy climbing a lamp post to take a shot of what I could photograph at best from the sidewalk, I gave it up," he explained in an interview with the writer Iva Pekárková for the magazine *Západ*. He did make one exception, however – when the newly-elected President of free Czechoslovakia, Václav Havel, flew into Washington in 1990.

Their meeting was arranged by Lukas's daughter Helena. When she heard that the new Czechoslovak President was coming to the USA, she found a number for the White House switchboard in the telephone directory and called it. She asked to be put through to the secretariat and announced that her father was well acquainted with Václav Havel, that he had acted as his guide during his trip to New York in 1968 and would very much like to be present again when the Czech President arrived. And so Jan Lukas documented Havel's visit to the White House, where he was received by President George Bush Sr., and also photographed Havel's famous speech to the US Congress.

Lukas made only two visits to Czechoslovakia after the Velvet Revolution – in autumn 1990 and in 1995. On the occasion of his eightieth birthday the Torst publishing house brought out Lukas's *Prague Diary*. At the book launch there were speeches by Lukas' friends the Minister of Culture Pavel Tigrid and the actor Jiří Suchý. The following day he was received at Prague Castle by Václav Havel and their meeting was photographed by Lukas' daughter Helena, who had decided to follow in her father's footsteps.

Ronald Reagan, 1972 (Photo Jan Lukas)

Michael Douglas, George Voskovec, Milos Forman (Photo Jan Lukas)

(131)

On the roof of Alexander Hammid's residence, New York. From left
Helena Lukas, Jan Lukas, Milena Lukas, Jana Lukas, Miloš Forman,
Ivan Passer, Jaroslav Papousek. (August 1966, photo Hella Hammid)

Václav Havel and Ferdinand Peroutka. (New York 1968,
photo Jan Lukas)

Crew of Apollo 11 visiting New York. (August 1969, photo Jan Lukas)

Václav Havel in US Congress (February 1990, photo Jan Lukas)

Preserve Memory

"We would see each other from time to time, sometimes we would write and once a month we would always speak on the phone," *Vendulka said as she sipped her tea, nonchalantly raising the little finger of her right hand. "Whenever I came to New York I would look him up in person. Sometimes we'd have dinner together. Honza invited me to his exhibitions and every year would send me an original greetings card. Wait a moment, I've stored them all in this drawer."* She got up briskly from her armchair and brought from the next room a yellow envelope on which was written Jan Lukas and family: New Year cards. Real life!!!

"Did you ever talk together about the past?" I asked.

"No, never. He respected the fact that I didn't want to go back over it. There were lots of other things that were more interesting for us to talk about. He didn't give up taking photographs until he was seriously ill. He even stopped sending new year's greetings. He died in the morning of 28 August 2006 from a stroke. Helena called to tell me. I was really sorry not to be able to go to his funeral. I had just had an operation on my spine and it wasn't possible."

Vendulka fell silent and a hush settled over the room.

I realised that the music had stopped playing a while ago.

"He was a real friend. I will always be grateful to him for what he did for me and my family."

She was evidently tired after talking for so long. It was time to say goodbye. Vendulka offered to drive me. I wanted to call a taxi, but she wouldn't hear of it. When she was dropping me off outside the hotel in the centre of Columbus, I asked her why she had finally decided to speak after refusing so many times. She switched off the engine and told me to listen carefully.

"I was never one of those who talk about it. I never kept a diary or even notes. I tried, but I didn't manage to. I was unable to describe my memories as I wanted to. Suddenly they seemed remote and detached, as if the girl I was talking about wasn't me. Before the war I led a fairy-tale life. I had loving parents, lots of friends, and my whole future ahead of me. And suddenly it all vanished. My Dad, the world I knew, and also a lot of myself, in fact. But it didn't disappear from my memory. My close relatives are still with me and I dream about them at night. I am always thinking about them, even though I don't let people see it. Even after all these years I still see my father – his smile, his face, I can feel him stroking my hair. And I can still picture moments I shared with my Mom. I have a vivid image of her coming in the evening to read me a story and pulling my eiderdown right up to my chin. And at the same time it is all mixed up with the horrible things that happened. I never stop asking myself, why was it me that survived? Why couldn't my Dad too?"

"Didn't your children ask you about it?" I broke in.

"In 1998 I took Christina to an exhibition where Honza's photo "Before the transport" was also on display. I warned her that she was going to see a photo on which she might recognise me. And then I learnt to my surprise that she was familiar with the photo, having come across it in photo collections – once in a book from my bookshelf and once in a book shop when we took a trip to Prague together. And so I started to tell her – and my other daughters – some things about the past, but never in detail. All my children were born and grew up on another continent, in America, far from my original homeland. I told myself it would be remote for them, and possibly make no sense. I didn't want to burden them. I thought I didn't have the right to offload my own suffering onto them."

"OK, but what impelled you to speak in the end?" I continued to press her.

"I finally decided that the only chance of preserving my recollections of my family, of who I was, of my parents and our identity, was to start talking about it."

In the months that followed, Vendulka and I were in regular contact. We talked on the phone and exchanged emails. I asked her for additional details of her story, but mostly we wrote about how the trees were blossoming in her garden, how she was enjoying resting in their shade, and about her and my children. In her last letter she mentioned that some friends were enticing her to spend a few days in Greece with them. She wrote that she would be only too pleased to make the trip, but she was too old for it. She died in the night of 1 July 2017 at her house in Columbus.

New life in America. Marriage with Alexander Hořava, Karla Voglová centre. (1953, archive of Hořava and Old families)

Vendulka with her second husband Jacob Wise Old, her children and her mother Karla. (USA, 1973, archive of Hořava and Old families)

"Don't make a big thing of it and write, OK?"
(Vendulka on one of her many trips, no date, archive
of Hořava and Old families)

What had been a distant dream in Terezín...

...came true. (Vendulka's costume designs, Columbus, no date, archive of Hořava and Old families)

(143)

Afterword

The memory of the places that Vendulka and her parents passed through during the war is fading. The family camp at Auschwitz was destroyed, only the foundations of the prison huts remain. Under the post-war settlement Christianstadt was assigned to Poland and is now known as Nowogród Bobrzański. Not a trace remained of the camp, which is now the location of a Polish army base. However, in the surrounding pine forests there are still scattered ruins of the Dynamit AG chemical works where Vendulka and her mother filled detonators. But all that remains of the factory are ruins covered in grass and moss.

Weisswasser in Germany has been transformed into an attractive town, lying just a few kilometres from the Polish frontier. When the camp was destroyed, family homes were built in its place. Children play in their front gardens and their parents have barbecues. The only reminder of the past is a monument unveiled in 2000. Attached to it is an iron plate engraved with a Jewish menorah and a brief notice that one of hundreds of sub-camps of the Gross-Rosen concentration camp stood there. In addition there is a quotation from the Jewish Nobel Peace Prize laureate Elie Wiesel: "There is no better path to tolerance and humanity than remembrance of that period, of the suffering of one single child, of the tears of one single mother."

Karla Voglová died in August 1985. She is buried in the New Jewish Cemetery in Prague along with her husband Šimon (Šimon only symbolically). Vendulka brought her mother's remains here during one of her trips to Prague. She later told her children that it didn't matter to her where she herself would be buried. They scattered her ashes partly in Columbus and partly in Prague.

Vendulka's friends from Terezín – Dáša and Líza – lived after the war in the USA where they married and had families. Like Vendulka they have since died. Kitty lived happily in Australia, among her family until she passed away in 2020.

Vendulka's friend Věra Glaserová, whom she met on the death march, emigrated to Canada after the war. Her memories of the war oppressed her so much that she threw herself into Niagara Falls, leaving behind three children. Her brother, who served in the RAF, perished at the end of the war in the wreckage of his plane.

Lukas's daughters Jana and Helena live in New York and return to Prague regularly.

Vendulka's children Susan, Kathy and Leigh live in Columbus, Christina lives in New York. They had a bench made, which stands in a quiet park in Columbus. It bears the label: "In memory of Hana Vendulka 'Wendy' Old. Remembered with love. Kindness was in her every step, love in every gesture."

Acknowledgements

I would like to thank Vlasta Urbanová, whose financial support enabled me to travel to the places connected with Vendulka's wartime experiences. Her offer was spontaneous and very warm-hearted. I am indebted to Vladimír Žežulka for accompanying me on my journey around Poland and Germany. He helped me find what was lost long ago. Thanks are due to my wife Lucie for her boundless patience and empathy. When writing my books I have always been fortunate with the choice of editor, and on this occasion I was particularly fortunate – Ondřej Nezbeda treated my text with exceptional care. Michaela Sidenberg of the Jewish Museum in Prague, Jan Mlčoch of the Museum of Applied Arts, and photography theorist Josef Moucha commented on the manuscript, and their observations were always most valuable. My thanks go to Nadia Rovderová of Art in Box gallery for her help with photographs. The book would never have appeared without the patient and unselfish assistance of Helena Lukas and Jana Dickerson in filling the gaps in their father's extraordinary life story. I am extremely grateful to Susan, Kathy and Christina, for their warm welcome in Columbus and New York. And my greatest thanks, of course, go to Vendulka. I will never cease to be grateful to her for telling me the story of her eventful life.

Literature

Adam Drda: Zvláštní zacházení: Rodinný tábor terezínských Židů v Auschwitz II. – Birkenau, *Revolver Revue* 2014

Eva Erbenová: *Sen*, Prague: Nakladatelství G plus G, 2001

Anita Franková, Anna Hyndráková, Věra Hájková, Františka Faktorová: *Svět bez lidských dimenzí – čtyři ženy vzpomínají*, Prague: Státní židovské muzeum v Praze, 1991

Benjamin Frommer: *National Cleansing: Retribution Against Nazi Collaborators in Postwar Czechoslovakia*, Cambridge: Cambridge University Press, 2005

Robert Gerwarth: *Poražení – Světová válka byla jen jedna*, Prague: Paseka, 2018

Jiří Kovtun: *Republika v nebezpečném světě – Éra prezidenta Masaryka 1918–1935*, Prague: Torst, 2005

Lucie Ondřichová: *Příběh Fredyho Hirsche*, Prague: Sefer – Institut Terezínské iniciativy, 2001

Tomáš Pěkný: Historie Židů v Čechách a na Moravě, Prague: Sefer, 2001

Timothy Snyder: *Bloodlands: Europe Between Hitler and Stalin*, New York: Basic Books, 2010

Rudolf Vrba: *Utekl jsem z Osvětimi*, Prague: Nakladatelství Federace židovských obcí, 2007